TO HELL, WITH THE IRS!

TO THE KINGDOM OF CHRIST, IT CANNOT COME!

STEVEN SEGO

Gotham Books

30 N Gould St.
Ste. 20820, Sheridan, WY 82801
https://gothambooksinc.com/

Phone: 1 (307) 464-7800

Published by Gotham Books (September 12, 2024)

ISBN: 979-8-88775-414-7 (P)
ISBN: 979-8-88775-415-4 (E)

Table of Contents

DISCLAIMER

Before you read this book, you are encouraged to check with your friends, your politicians, your clergy, your relatives, your attorney and anyone else you think will tell you the truth, or who you think is smarter than you, to give you an honest and unbiased opinion. You need to know that everything I say in this book is simply my opinion, and there are many people who may disagree with my conclusions, and findings.

If you do anything I recommend, without the supervision of a licensed attorney, you do so at your own risk. The publisher, the author, the distributors, and bookstores, present this information for educational purposes only.

I am not an attorney, nor do I claim to be, nor am I attempting to practice law without a license. This book is only my opinions, my thoughts, and my conclusions based on sound knowledge, and/or experience. The information in this book is for educational purposes only, and you, and only you, are responsible, if you so choose to do anything based on what you read in this book.

Steven Sego

FOREWORD
About the Book

This book is written for the purpose of educating the freedom loving people, who believe in God, and are aware of the evil the IRS represents. It is my intentions to educate the people with the knowledge of understanding the IRS, enabling them to make educated and deliberate decisions in dealing with this dishonest agency.

I, the author have already walked the walk, and talked the talk, but ultimately, everyone will have to walk this same walk, in order to acquire their freedom. Freedom is not free. In all cases Freedom requires a price be paid, but the purpose of this book is to help make it so much understandable and simpler. The main point is to keep Christ as the center of your focus, because that is where we all hope to end up, is where he is at.

It is my prayer that all people will believe in Christ and not fear. He has told us 365 times in the Bible to not fear. We just need to have knowledge and understand. This is the main purpose of this book, to help others understand.

I have taken the first chapter from my previous book, "Two Churches Only", as a fitting beginning to this book, as I explain and show proof of how simple understanding the IRS is. Hopefully, by the end of it, people will begin to realize how they have been robbed by the IRS for years. There are several reasons this could happen. They either trust their government and believe that they wouldn't lie to them, or some church leader, acting as blind guides, are telling them, that to be Christian, is to do everything their government tells them to do. They tell them it is for their own good. Possibly the people are too gullible, or lazy to search out the truth for themselves. By reading this book all of the way through, is an important step to freeing yourself from the chains of bondage, and getting closer to God.

ACKNOWLEDGMENTS

I would like to recognize and acknowledge those who have inspired me in this work, but mainly, first and foremost, I recognize my God, and Father in Heaven, for bringing me up out of discouraging and frustrating circumstances and situations, and for giving me the knowledge and the fortitude to stand tall.

I also recognize my beautiful and good wife, Davina, for her relentless and unwavering support throughout the years, some of which have been hard and trying times. God has certainly blessed me, when he sent her into my life. I also recognize and acknowledge my great children whom I love dearly, especially my immediate children: Stevana, Jordan, Olivia, and Grace. It is for this specific purpose, in building this bridge, figuratively speaking, that I am writing this book, in hopes to give the ones who read it, a little more insight into what it will be like when facing eternity.

I also acknowledge other friends and family members, and all of those good people out there searching for knowledge, and understanding. You know who you are, as there are too many to name. All of you are the ones I wrote this book for, hopefully to inspire you all, to finish the race standing up, and strong in the faith of God, to the end, that we will all be together, in the Kingdom of our Heavenly Father, and His Son Jesus Christ.

I especially am thankful to my oldest daughter, Stevana, for her art work on the cover of this book. She has truly been a great help and stalwart in helping me accomplish my work.

INTRODUCTION
About the Author

I graduated from Noxon High School in 1976, from Noxon, Montana. From there I went on a mission for the Church of Jesus Christ of Latter-Day Saints, to Hong Kong, China in 1977-1979, where I learned the Chinese dialect of Cantonese, and taught the gospel of Jesus Christ in this dialect. Upon my return from Hong Kong, I attended Ricks College, in Rexburg, Idaho, for a short time.

In 1980, I married a girl from the Church, who happened to be of a liberal mindset, and therefore found myself unequally yoked, as I was of a conservative upbringing. The marriage didn't last but ten years, but of this union, five beautiful children were born. These combined with the four children from the preceding marriage is what has inspired me to write this book.

In 1992 I married a beautiful, smart woman from Northern Ireland, who became a naturalized American citizen, March 21, 2019. We raised four beautiful, intelligent children, all of whom are grown and doing well in the faith of Jesus Christ. In this same year I got involved with an educational group called the "Concerned Citizens for Constitutional Government of Idaho". This is where I really began to learn knowledge. As I worked for the welfare of my family, and learning about our government, and doing what I knew to be right, God has opened my eyes, to what the real truth really is. My eyes were made to see, and God has opened my understanding.

There are several people who have crossed my path throughout the years, with different insights, knowledge, and understandings which has helped me greatly, and influenced my thinking process, and has helped to make me into a better man. I thank God for all of these good people.

I am getting older now, far from the young man of 35, when I was learning knowledge by hard knocks, and having to be resilient and able to bounce back. I have come through much trial and experience, and I want my loved ones to have the benefit of my learning experiences and knowledge of them. Everyone only has one chance at this life, and it is my desire to help the next generation along, as well as the ones who are pressing forward now, and so I have written this book to perhaps make it easier for the ones coming behind me to find their way towards God and Freedom.

I was inspired to write this book because I love my family, especially my children coming along searching for answers. There are certain things that have inspired me throughout the years and I see myself as I get older, my ability to get around is lessening, my eyes are becoming more dim, my hearing is fading, my memory shorter, and I am loosing teeth, etc.. Because of this, I find it necessary to put my knowledge, for their benefit on paper. I have done this, for them to use as a resource material, to help them along the pathway of life,

I see myself as a bridge builder and I want to share the last eight lines of my favorite poem with the reader, as it should apply to us all. This poem was also the favorite poem of my father, Raymond Sego, who had it memorized and quoted it often. This Poem is entitled:

"The Bridge Builder"

"...The builder lifted his old grey head.

Good friend, in the path I have come," he said,

There followeth after me today

A youth whose feet must pass this way.

This chasm that has been naught to me

To that fair-haired youth may a pitfall be.

He, too, must cross in the twilight dim;

Good friend, I am building the bridge for him."

By Will Allen Dromgoole.

I feel an obligation to my God and fellowman to spread the truth along the way, and warn the people, otherwise, I would not like myself, and would not be doing a service to God or my brothers and sisters out there in this dreary world. We must remember that there is a life after this one, and this one is only a test. In this world we are fighting against principalities and powers of darkness. We are choosing which king we want to be aligned with for eternity. I choose Christ the almighty king, and knowing and acting against the lies and deceptions of worldly agencies and governments, makes us more likely to be unselfish and free. The IRS is a system of slavery, so if we expect to be in the Kingdom of Christ, then how can we expect to deserve it, while looking back and seeing our families and fellowmen existing in Hell, when we could have prevented some of it by just opening our mouths,

The things that I have written in this book are true, and I have lived what I am telling the reader. Now it is up to each child of God to seek after him in faith and understanding. Receive the gospel of Jesus Christ, so that you can be numbered among the sons and daughters of God, and some day see him as he is. I can't explain the truth about the IRS any plainer than this. Anyone in this battle, have my most heartfelt understanding, and my prayers go with you big-time, but don't fear, because it is really very simple, once you understand who you are. God loves you, and so do I.

Sincerely, Steven Sego.

CHAPTER 1
The Internal Revenue Service

Growing up, as a young man, my Dad was very conservative and had a love of God. He took his children to church every Sunday, almost without fail, unless something happened beyond his control, such as a sickness or car breaking down.

The ones I looked up to were my older brothers, who had some knowledge, but not a lot about what was happening in our government, such as how elected officials were deviating from the Constitution, and attacking our unalienable rights. They knew enough to notice the erosion of morality, and the enhanced oppression being perpetrated a little at a time by left leaning elected officials, which were many. They regularly voiced their concerns and opinions, and I listened to the best of my ability, because these things interested me, as I was trying to gain knowledge and grow physically and spiritually.

As it were, my being raised on sound principles of the gospel, I learned not to take someone's opinion as always the truth, but I learned to question everything, until I was satisfied I had arrived at the truth, as I was wanting to make a difference to God and for my country.

In 1992 I got involved with a group called "The Concerned

Citizens for Constitutional Government of Idaho". The group's intent was to educate the public about the erosion of Constitutional rights being perpetrated by elected officials, including: Presidents, Congressmen and women, judges, mayors, governors etc. I began to see that, "we the people," were being lied to consistently in a deliberate manner, and that there were very few elected officials in fiduciary positions that the people could trust.

There are many, seriously, bad laws put into place by left leaning Republican and Democrat left leaning, liberal presidents, congressmen and women, trying to little, by little destroy America from within. The purpose of this Chapter is to expose the fraudulent IRS, and explain who and what they represent.

There have been a lot of books and literature written, related to the fraudulent nature and practices of the Internal Revenue Service, or simpler terms, the IRS. My goal is to simplify the persons' understanding of why the IRS exists, and how they exist, but in other words, why we the people let them exist. If the people would simply wake up, and show some fortitude, the IRS would not exist.

The IRS is, simply put, the muscle man of the Federal Reserve Bank. The Federal Reserve Bank is the most evil institution that ever existed on the Planet Earth. The money system throughout history, when corrupted, has caused the destruction of all nations after enslaving the people, and causing misery and bankruptcy.

When private business and people control the creation of money, which is to serve as the exchange of goods and services, then it is easy for conflict of interest, selfish ambition, bribery, and control of the populace, to take place. The Federal Reserve has extended its power across the globe, with the intent of controlling governments.

America is the "little horn" that wounded the beast almost to death, and it has been plotted by Satan, for 100's of years, if not 1000"s of years, to heal the wound of the beast, by destroying America. It is no accident that the Democrats are busy attempting to obstruct President Trump from "Making America Great Again". One of the primary means for doing this and ruling the world, is the creation of the Federal Reserve Bank. Mayer Amschel Rockefeller stated: "Permit me to issue and control the money of a nation, and I care not who makes its laws!" Make no mistake about it, these evil people care not about America, but they care only about power.

The problem for these evil, Anti-America and Anti-God people, is that America is filled with Freedom and God loving patriots, who have knowledge, are armed, and will stand up and fight if they have to, aggressively, fearlessly, and committed to the cause of Freedom. I am one of these, and I am going to reveal the truth and simplicity of the evil IRS.

Up to 1992, I was ignorant of the IRS's fraud, until I was presented with a video tape by a man named Stewart. This video showed a man named Carter, and his fight with the IRS. It struck me so hard, as to find out how blatantly the IRS would lie, to rob this man of his money, and then lie to cover up a lie. They were caught with their hands in the cookie jar, and ever since, I have refused to file, or pay the IRS one red cent. I haven't filed since 1993, and when your lights finally go on, you will never file again either.

Most people today, suffer from a terrible disease called "ignorance". This disease can be accidentally or on purpose. Most people are ignorant because they don't get involved in politics, or government, where they would learn Constitutional principles, because they don't want to go to the trouble. The rest claim they are smart, but won't get involved because they are either trying to cover their own selfish lusts or desires, or they would much rather play the stupid card, or because they are afraid.

The Constitution allows for three lawful taxes only, and they are: Import taxes, Export taxes, and Excise Taxes. That means that the "income tax" is not lawful. In 1913, Colonel House, while under the Woodrow Wilson administration, stood before congress and announced: "it appears that the 16th Amendment has been ratified". The wording is, "it appears". This is how magicians deceive others, into making others believe something that is not real, to appear real. It is sleight of hand or deception. This is what Colonel House did, to get the people to believe that the 16th Amendment was made law. Would you honestly believe a lying Democrat? That is all the language the Democrats know how to speak. They speak the language of the Devil, and that is lies, along with some choice GOP or Republican traitors.

The following is taken from the "Federal Civil Judicial Procedure and Rules, 1997 Edition. "Article XVI of the Constitution", "The Congress shall have power to lay and collect taxes on **incomes**, from whatever source derived, without apportionment among the several States, and without regard to any census or enumeration." Further included are "Historical Notes", "Proposal and Ratification". *"The Sixteenth Amendment, set out in 36 Stat. 184, was proposed to the legislatures of the several States by the Sixty-First Congress, on July 12, 1909, and was declared, in a proclamation by the Secretary of State, dated February 25, 1913, to have been ratified."*

One needs to notice the word play "Incomes". The word "income" is something Foreign Earned. Also the word play on, "from whatever source derived". From whatever foreign source, they failed to explain. The Sixteenth Amendment was just declared as to appearing to be ratified by a "Bully" Democrat lead Congress, just like when the Congress tried to push through the impeachment of Donald Trump.

If you are a Naturalized citizen, domiciled within one of the several states, or Natural Born citizen and not receiving Foreign Earned Income, then the Sixteenth Amendment does not apply to you. If your employment is with a corporation within the United

States, and you are a natural born or naturalized citizen of the "United States" of America, it still does not apply to you, because the money you earn is "remuneration", where you are trading your assets, (your labor), for value in like kind, as exchange. Further, it does not apply to you because they offer a fraudulent form for you to fill out, (1040), which carries a penalty of ten years in prison for mail-fraud, and they can't force you to commit a crime. Therefore, you have no "incoming" source of remuneration.

Even though it may appear to some people that the states ratified the 16th Amendment, since to tax your source of remuneration is not Constitutional, then, is all they can do is tax foreign earned incoming monies, from whatever source, and even then, it is a "voluntary compliance" system.

A man named Bill Benson wrote a book called "The Law that Never Was". He went to every state in the union and did the research, and learned that not one single state ratified the 16th Amendment. He documented the results, and put them together in this book, and published his conclusions. His findings were, that not one single state ratified the 16th Amendment. Some people try to say that some states ratified it, but that it wasn't done properly. The important point to remember, is this: that, if the 16th Amendment wasn't ratified properly, well then, it wasn't ratified!! It wasn't ratified properly, because it was not done by the people, or for the people, and therefore it's not Constitutional!! The 16th Amendment therefore, is not positive law, but only "prima facie law". This means, it is law until proven otherwise. Bill Benson's conclusions just proved, otherwise.

Whether or not the States ratified the 16th Amendment, one fundamental principle still remains, that it doesn't apply to the "Sovereign Citizen". The wording of this Amendment was sculpted for the "United States Citizen"/Corporate citizens/persons/foreigners etc., by the Federal Government, for the Federal Government, and not by "We The People". Steps to remember in understanding the IRS are these:

1).   If the 16th Amendment is not really law, and if it was, would only apply to corporate citizens of the federal United States. So then having to file income taxes is not enforceable by law within the several united states of America-Republic. Anything then, that the Federal Reserve and the IRS throw at you is 100% not legal, but is a fraud. It is a law on appearance only, until proven otherwise.

Friday, March 4, 1994, Judge David Hagen, of the Federal District Court in Reno, Nevada, issued the following "Declaratory Judgment that: a) The 16th Amendment was and is invalid: b) The Federal Reserve Act of 1913, is declared Unconstitutional as it was and is applied to State Citizens: c) The Gold Reserve Act of 1934 to be a fraud on its surface and to be declared Unconstitutional: d) Title 26 USC (the Internal Revenue Code) to apply to the Federal United States, (not to the citizens of the fifty states) and all other implications to be fraud and therefore declared Unconstitutional." *Ronald L. Jackson v. United States, et al, Case No: CV-N-93-401-DWH.*

2). The further a person digs into the IRS, they begin to realize and uncover the fact that Title 26 USC, the Internal Revenue Code, only pertains to immigration; including nonresidents, permanent residents, resident aliens, illegal aliens, federal residents, corporations, trusts, etc.. It does not apply or include Natural Born citizens, or Naturalized citizens under the Constitution of the United States of America, or of the several United States of America. These Constitutional Citizens are Exempt from any federal or state income tax.

The "Remedy in Law" is Uniform Commercial Codes 1-207/1-308, and 1-103. This Remedy can be used very effectively when signing your W-2 forms, or W-4, when being employed by an employer. I would simply write in my name, my address, my social security number. Nothing else, except down at the bottom, the form asks if you are exempt. On the W-4 down at Number: "7 I claim exemption from withholding for (year), and I certify that I meet **both** of the following conditions for exemption." Both of these conditions are: "Last year I had a right to a refund of **all** federal income tax withheld because I had **no** tax liability, **and** this year I expect a refund of **all** federal income tax withheld because I expect to have **no** tax liability." If you are a natural born citizen, or naturalized citizen of America-Republic, then you meet both of these criteria, and can honestly say you are "Exempt".

A "natural born citizen" is someone born into the country, as natural as creation. The "naturalized citizen" is someone who has become like the natural born citizen, through going through the process of becoming a full-fledged citizen of the united states of America-Republic. They have become one with the "natural born" citizen, and the same under the "God of nature" and "nature's God". This is like "baptism". To receive the "gospel of Jesus Christ and being baptized, makes you one with Christ, and puts you on the same plain as those who have been Christians all of their lives."

This is simply due to the fact that you are a natural born citizen, or a naturalized citizen, and income taxes don't apply to a citizen under the Constitution. What I did, was write in the box at the bottom right, EXEMPT, then I signed it at the bottom left. Before I signed it, However, I wrote just above where my signature would be: "Not Liable! UCC 1-207/1-308 & UCC 1-103". What I am saying is this: I refuse to be forced to perform under any unknown contract that I have not entered into knowingly, and I also refuse the liability of the compelled benefit! The income tax is an unknown contract.

Since 1938, our Common Law has been replaced by Commercial Law, and most of us today, were not around in 1938. We were not even a twinkle in our daddy's eye. We were not alive or of age at the time of this contract, so it is unknown to us and is covered by the remedy of UCC 1-207/1-308. What information was once only in UCC 1-207, has now been moved to UCC 1-308, but to be sure I included everything, I write it UCC 1-207/1-308. This is so as to avoid any trickery. UCC 1-103; means that we refuse to be liable for the compelled benefit. The compelled benefit is the Fiat money system. The money is not real, and this fake money is I.O.U.'s of the Federal Reserve, once again another unknown contract. UCC 1-103 is our remedy for not being liable for this fake money, being as we were not around or of age to agree to it, or of age to contract. Any document pertaining to demand of money by any government agency, such as court fees or fines, jail fees, booking fees, etc. can also have this remedy when used.

3). There are no "Implementing Regulations" attached to the 16th Amendment, or to Title 26 USC, compelling or requiring the Constitutional/natural born/naturalized Citizen to file Income Taxes. Any positive law, is accompanied with implementing regulations, compelling performance, and a penalty for nonperformance. Any regulation associated with the 1040 Form is referenced to Alcohol, Tobacco and Firearms.

4). The Income Tax is a "self-assessment and voluntary compliance system". Based upon the "Handbook For Special Agents", "criminal investigation intelligence division, Internal Revenue Service", states: "Agents"..."Our tax system is based on individual self-assessment and **voluntary compliance... the**

material contained in this handbook is confidential in character...and must not under any circumstance be made available to persons outside the service". By, **"Mr. Mortimer Caplin, Internal Revenue Service, Commissioner."**

The IRS does not personally send you or anyone you know, any form through the mail, unless explicitly requested in writing and signed by you. Instead, they want you to voluntarily, go to any library, courthouse, or post office, and pick one up. They then expect you to fill it out, or pay to have it done, with your own name, social security number, then sign it with your signature, put your own stamp on the envelope, seal the envelope yourself, address it, then drop it in the mail to send to them. You have just sent a demand or request to the IRS with the intention of receiving a monetary benefit. What the IRS doesn't tell you, is that you have just requested this monetary benefit on a fraudulent form, and sent this request through the mail, committing mail fraud.

5).   The 1040 Form is a fraudulent document. The IRS would not send it to you in the mail, but you send it to them demanding payment for money, and now you have just committed "mail fraud". The masses are committing mail fraud every year unknowingly, but the IRS keeps quiet about it, because they are able to rob the people, because of the people's ignorance, and they are serving their master, the Federal Reserve Bank.

Though the IRS doesn't want to alarm the masses, they target those who act like they do know, and if those who know, cause trouble for them by trying to educate others, they will try and frame such a person by lies and deceit in such a way, as to show the person committed mail fraud and tax evasion voluntarily. These are two separate felonies, with the penalties being 10 years in prison, each.

Title 26 CFR: 602.101 fails to cross-reference the IRS form 1040 (OMB Control Number 1545-0074) for the purpose of collecting information from the public, necessary to enforce CFR: 1.1-1.

6). The IRS is not part of the Federal Government, but is a private corporation since 1933, when they were first incorporated in the State of Delaware. They are now headquartered in the federal territory of Puerto Rico. Title 26 IRC itself, supports the fact that the term "United States" is being used in the "geographic sense", and thus refers only to the District of Columbia, and territories over which the federal government has exclusive jurisdiction, but not the several states. (see IRC: 770(a)(9)-(10), (see also Caha v. United States 152 US 211 and Foley Brothers v. Filardo 336 US 281 (1948).

It has also been stated by the Supreme Court that each of the several states is a foreign country, as to the District of Columbia and, thus, maintains exclusive jurisdiction within its' geographic area. This is why The IRS, is no longer headquartered in the several United States, but is now in Puerto Rico, a territory. They have no jurisdiction within the several states unless you give it to them.

7).   The IRS works as a collection agency for the Federal Reserve Bank, which, is also a private corporation and also not a part of our Federal Government. This is another deception, by the use of the word, "Federal".

8).   There is no law requiring a person to file a 1040 Form, or requiring a person to file any unlawful income tax for that matter. For the IRS to try and force someone to file a 1040 Form, is the same as attempting to force the person to commit a felony. They want the person to file the form voluntarily.

9).   To file income taxes do not apply to Natural Born or Naturalized Citizens under the Constitution of the United States, and has the commercial remedy in UCC 1-207/1-308 &UCC 1-103. Remember this: income is for those who make money from without the several United States Republic. Foreign earned income is what is taxable. It is incoming money from a foreign source. To call yourself a sovereign citizen under the Constitution, is one country. A corporation of the United States of America, is another, or foreign country. The IRS does not want to explain the term: "INCOME", but this is what it is. They do not want to have to tell you their meaning, otherwise it would reveal the truth. If you are a sovereign citizen, then the proper term to use is: "REMUNERATION".

10).   The IRS is a system of threat, duress, and coercion. So much so, that companies and corporations are intimidated into acting as agents for collecting from their employees, by withholding

13

from their employee's paychecks. The businesses and corporations, are not agents and not under any law to act as collection agents for the IRS. All that is required in order for the businesses or corporations to qualify their actions, is to give each employee the option, to voluntarily fill out the W-4 or W-2, with any exemptions they assess themselves as having, then send the completed W-4, or W-2 to the IRS, and at the end of the year, furnish to the employee a 1099 or, with the statement of the employees' earnings for the year, and that is all.

11).   The IRS has no police, or law enforcement powers. They can only lie, threaten, intimidate, misrepresent, and deceive people into doing their dirty work. They scheme and watch for a crime to be committed, such as, setting a person up for mail fraud and /or tax evasion, then they make a complaint to the correct authorities, and have you indicted, or arrested, tried and convicted, but of themselves and their evil agency, they have no police power.

So you see, the IRS has no power at all, unless you give them the power over you. They have no jurisdiction over a natural born or naturalized citizen of the United States Of America Republic. In order for the IRS to have jurisdiction over you, you must be in the water with them, where they can harm you. A letter from Harry Reid, on US Senate letter head, replied to an inquiry to a Mr. Tolotti, and said: "I consulted the legal and tax divisions of the Congressional Research Service to answer your question. They found no tax on an "occupation of Common Right."

When growing up, and in school, we as children were taught about the Constitution of the United States of America, and about our rights under it, and how we are protected, because of this special, sacred document. This is the government of the "Republic" of America that we pledged allegiance to every morning before beginning school, while in grade school growing up. I have made comparison as to the Constitution, as representing dry land, or Common Law Jurisdiction.

Another system not explained to the people, are the laws under Maritime Law or Old Merchant Law. This Maritime Law is the law of the sea. On the ocean, in a ship, the captain is the dictator, with absolute authority and control. What he says goes, in the way he manages his ship. In Washington D.C., or the District of Columbia, this same jurisdiction is prevalent. This is called Admiralty Jurisdiction. By incorporating our businesses, and churches, has brought this system onto the dry land, and out of the District of Columbia, where it was told to stay.

The oceanic laws/Uniform Commercial Codes, another name for Admiralty Jurisdiction, have replaced Common law back in 1938, under Erie versus Tompkins. In the respective states, they have been codified into state codes, such as in Wisconsin, they are Wisconsin Code. In Idaho, they are Idaho Code, etc...So because of this maritime law, or commercial law on the land, we need the remedy in UCC 1-207/1-308, and UCC 1-103, in order to maintain our Common Law Rights under the Constitution.

In any system, the people of God must have a choice, of whom they wish to serve. Though the commercial law is intimidating, free choice must also be made available. The evil Democrats and left, leaning GOP. or evil agencies won't tell us where the remedies are, therefore, we must read, study, find, and understand for ourselves, where the key is, that unlocks the door of our freedom.

The Federal Reserve money system, makes slaves of the people worldwide. The Fiat or fake money is made by it, and it is a private corporation. The Federal Reserve owns these I.O.U.'s, and you are in debt just by having it in your possession, and it must be paid back with interest, and to make sure you pay it back, it sends its collection agency, to intimidate, threaten, coerce, deceive etc., whatever it takes. Because the IRS is out of the sea of commercial law, and onto the dry land, under constitutional law, it is completely powerless.

We all need to understand, that in America today, the Constitution is the "Supreme Law" of the land, and is a representation of God. When close to God, we are safe, but when we partake of that other system of government/"fictional-foreign" system of government, or Maritime law, we come under another foreign jurisdiction. Admiralty Jurisdiction is its name, among others. It is Contract Law. Other names already mentioned earlier, are Federal, Corporate, King, Dictator, Fascist, Socialist,

Communist, or Democracy. Other Bible, or ancient terms are: Babylon, Egypt, The World, Whore of all the Earth, Great and Abominable Church. These are all different terms, but they all mean the same thing.

Another analogy is this: Imagine the IRS as a gigantic Octopus. In Puget Sound, in Seattle, there are some huge ones. In old times, there were old stories handed down about sea monsters attacking ships. A good example of this is "2000 Leagues Under The Sea". Some of the pictures show huge tentacles wrapped around the ships, threatening to capsize their boats. As long as those Octopuses stay in the water, they are very scary monsters. Now take that monster sized Octopus and drop him on dry land, and you have nothing but a big blob of slimy, writhing tissue, which is completely helpless and powerless.

The water represents the law of the sea, or Admiralty Jurisdiction. The Land represents the Constitution or Common Law Jurisdiction. The IRS represents the scary, monstrous octopus, and when you take this evil agency out of the water and drop it under the Constitution, on the land, it becomes helpless, and powerless, and it will eventually die. This is really how simple it is. Each tentacle of the Octopus is a representation of what makes up the authority of the **"Beast".** 1) 16th Amendment wasn't ratified, or doesn't apply to the "natural" citizen, as having jurisdiction over the natural born or naturalized citizen; 2) There are no implementing regulations;

3) Title 26, the internal revenue code applies only to immigration, or federal agencies of the District of Columbia and not the several united states; 4) The system is a voluntary compliance system; 5) There is no law requiring a person to file; 6) The form 1040 used for gathering information from the public is a fraudulent form; 7) The IRS is not part of the Federal Government, but is a private corporation: 8) The IRS is a system of Intimidation; 9) The IRS has no police or enforcement powers.

So, knowing all of these things, just causes any authority the IRS appears to have, to just up and melt away, when it is overshadowed by the Constitution. The IRS is a system of Threat, Duress, and Coercion.

The United States of America is the correct name of our great "Republic". There is another corporate name given by evil people seeking to bring about the downfall of our Republic, and that is "The United States of America". This sleight of hand, or deception was made deliberately by the democrats/liberals trying to turn our Republic into a communist/socialist country, under Admiralty Jurisdiction. You can hear Nancy Pelosi, or any of the liberals talking about their "Democracy", and how they are trying to protect our "Democracy". Many of the GOP are just as guilty, such as George H.W. Bush, as he was publicly trying to usher in the New World Order of things. What they aren't telling you, and what they really mean, is that when they use this word, or title loosely, they are

TO HELL, WITH THE IRS!
TO THE KINGDOM OF CHRIST IT CANNOT COME!

claiming a Socialist government, and are trying the deception trick to get Americans to buy into it, after all, it does resemble a democratic form of government. However, democracy and democratic are two different things.

Democratic, is the form of government where the people are able to elect their own representatives, whether it is a Democracy or a Republic. The difference here is, that under a Republic, the elections are by the people, for the people, and of the people, and any, and everyone has equality and justice under the laws of the Constitution, and anyone can run for office. In a Democracy, the only choices you have for elected representatives, are from among the rich people. Only the rich rule, and are allowed to elect their leaders, masters, thus, making the poor and ordinary people chattel, like it was during the feudal system.

I have an old encyclopedia, published in 1890. It just happens to be the "D" volume. I looked up the term "Democracy", and right next to this word, in brackets, "Socialism". It explained that the term democracy is an old Greek form of government, where the people choose their leaders by election, but the catch is, that the rich are the only ones allowed to vote, because the chattel don't know what is best for themselves, so they are represented by the rich. This system would then allow the rich to be unchecked, they could manipulate, and even commit voter fraud, like they have done in the 2020 election. Donald J. Trump won the election by a landslide, and the evidence of "voter fraud" was deliberate and so obvious that the whole world can see it.

This is what the socialists, or communists are trying to do today. They want this form of government, they want a King over the land, they want power and riches, and control and they want we, the people to be their slaves, and deliver us back over to the corporate system, even the Roman Empire ruled by the Catholic Church.

The Mormon's, <u>Book of Mormon</u>, talks about "Gadianton Robbers", a secret criminal organization like the illuminati. This book also talks about "Kingmen", and all of these are who the Democrats are, and those who are liberals, parading around in Republican's clothing. *"42. And it came to pass that the wicked part of the people began again to build up the **secret oaths and combinations of Gadianton.**" (4 Nephi 1:42, Book of Mormon)*

*"1. And it came to pass that those who were desirous that Pahoran should be dethroned from the judgment-seat were called **kingmen**, for they were desirous that the law should be altered in a manner to overthrow the **free government** and to establish a king over the land." "6. And those who were desirous that Pahoran should remain chief judge over the land took upon them the name of **freemen;** and thus was the division among them, for the freemen had sworn or **covenanted to maintain their rights** and the privileges of their religion by a **free government.**" "7. And it came to pass that this matter of their contention was **settled by the voice of the people**,*

*And it came to pass that the voice of the people came in favor of the freemen, and Pahoran retained the judgment-seat, which caused much rejoicing among the brethren of Pahoran and also many of the **people of liberty**, who also put the king-men to silence, that they durst not oppose but were obliged to maintain **the cause of freedom.**" "8. Now those who were in favor of **kings were those of high birth**, and they sought **to be kings;** and they were supported by those **who sought power and authority over the people.**" (Alma 51:5-8, Book of Mormon)*

So, basically, America is split into two separate countries. Though we are citizens/sovereign of The American Republic, but are employed by a corporation, then the IRS looks on this like we are receiving foreign earned income, even though we are under the Constitution. They want to deceive you into believing that they have jurisdiction, even though they don't.

If you assert your rights, under the Constitution, then you are with God and under the Republic, country of America. You can work and receive remuneration from any lawful source, including corporations, and any amount, this includes capital gains. If, however, you have selfish desires, and wish to remain ignorant, and uphold lies and bad laws, like the IRS and its 16th Amendment, Roe v. Wade etc., then you are supporting Socialism/Democracy. I can't explain it any simpler than this.

The beauty of it all, is that, as we learn, gain knowledge, and grow, we have the ability to change, hopefully for the good, before we die, as we prepare to meet God, with our freedom intact, believing and accepting Christ as our Savior. Our change must be sincere, with commitment. We cannot sit on the fence in a lukewarm state, because God will spew us out of his mouth. *"15. I know thy works, that thou art neither cold nor hot: I would thou wert cold or hot." "16. So then because thou art* **lukewarm**, *and neither cold nor hot, I will spue thee out of my mouth." (Revelation 3:15-16, KJV)* In other words, if you won't stand for truth, then God won't have you. He will surrender you to the Devil's jurisdiction. God wants you to choose.

The last year I have ever filed was in 1993. Since then, it has been very educational. It was peaceful enough, until someone made an anonymous phone call to the mighty IRS. I have my suspicions as to who it was, but this started my educational journey contending with the Scary Octopus.

I battled the IRS from 1994-2001. I wrote an article to the "Idaho Observer" and the editor, Don Harkins, then ran it unedited, in my own words, and I am including it here, as I told it then, in July of 2001. Don wrote an introduction to my article in his own words, referring to the IRS:

"It cannot answer important questions. It simply goes from house to house; from business to business threatening to take peoples' property and put them in jail if they don't pay the protection

money they call income tax. Steve Sego and his wife Davina of Rathdrum chose to stand up to the IRS and seem to have battled the federal monster to a standstill. What program did they use? What method do they employ? They confronted the IRS head on, asked the right questions and stood up in truth and faith, the following account should be an inspiration to us all."

Titled: **"One family's confrontation with the IRS" by Steven Sego**

In 1994 I quit filing Income tax returns and I notified the Tax Commissioner in Washington D.C. by mail, telling her I was ashamed of her, and that I would no longer be filing tax returns.

I started getting letters telling me of a tax-deficiency, and that I needed to file 1040s. I replied with letters, always in a timely manner, declaring my sovereignty and upholding my Constitutional Rights. Of course, the Internal Revenue Agents were deaf and still kept on a coming. Consequently, the correspondence between them and me has filled seven big notebooks full of documentation.

In my investigations about the income tax I have learned that: (1) the Constitution was God's Law and; (2) The IRS was telling lies.

I made up my mind that I was going to obey God's Law. I bumbled and stumbled and made mistakes, but kept a steady prayer life to my Father in Heaven and observed to do all that I could, by learning the truth and then exercising what I knew to be true.

This has been a learning process and I have made mistakes. But I and my family are living testimonies that by going forward in truth and unafraid will lead to things working out for the best. I know that my knowledge and understanding of the IRS and what the truth really is has grown tremendously, and I am so grateful to my Heavenly Father for that.

In 1998 the IRS recorded In Kootenai County, a "Notice of Federal Tax Lien". I thought about what was going on and with a little more reading I ran across a document put out by the IRS that said anyone could visit any IRS office and the IRS would be happy to answer tax related questions.

So I did. I decided to go after the IRS and not wait for them to come after me. I called up my friend Herb Miles and asked him if he would like to go with me to visit the IRS because I had some questions I want to ask them. Herb agreed to meet me at their office. And so began my harassment of the IRS.

Our first meeting:

I had come upon some material where it appeared that something had been omitted from evidence, making an incomplete document and I wanted to ask the IRS about it. I wanted to put them on the spot. Herb and I met at the IRS office in Coeur d' Alene. We went up to the big steel door. We rang the doorbell, and after a minute a voice on the other side asked who we were and what we wanted. I told them that I was there to see a certain IRS agent (who was the supervisor for the Coeur d' Alene Office) the voice said just a minute. Pretty soon the door opened and a person opened the door and showed us to a room where we could wait for the agent.

Shortly the IRS agent appeared and asked what this was concerning. I told him that I had some questions. He told me that I needed an appointment, because it was apparent that he didn't know what to do with me on such short notice. However, I pulled out my paper, it being the IRS's own literature, stating that is all I had to do if I had any questions was to come down to any office of the IRS, and they would be glad to answer them.

I asked him if the paper was true. He said okay what do you want to know. I started asking him questions about the omissions of paragraphs and words from IRS material which made the documents incomplete. He didn't want to answer these questions and so he tried to take control of the meeting.

I reminded him that I had called the meeting and that I had the questions and that he needed to provide the answers. He told me that he didn't have to answer any questions. I asked him if the IRS regards themselves as public servants or not. He said that they do. I said if you are the servant then I am the master and you will answer any question that I ask. I also reminded him that if he didn't answer my questions I would keep coming back until I got them answered.

Herb and I had taken recorders, but this particular agent, would not let us record then, but we scheduled a meeting two weeks later telling him that we would be bringing recorders and witnesses.

The IRS agent, told another IRS agent living in Idaho Falls, Idaho about the visit he received from us. This other agent then called me and said that I didn't need to bother the first agent and that if I had any questions concerning my account that I had to deal with him.

He also informed me that he could meet with me on January 7, 1999. I wrote back to the agent in Idaho Falls and told him that I accept the meeting gladly. I also reminded him that I called the meeting, and that he was the servant and that I will be asking the questions. I told him that when he came, to be sure and bring some documents with him. I wanted him to produce the contractual agreement that I made with the IRS, if it is true that I do have an account with them. I also wanted him to provide the statute which accompanied the implementing regulations. I added, I will be bringing two tape recorders and three witnesses.

Our second meeting:

The meeting took place as planned, and the agent from Idaho Falls for the IRS had his own tape recorder. I piled into him demanding now to produce the documents I had requested that he bring with him prior to the meeting. The only thing that he pulled out was the statute on Individual taxes. I asked him where the contract that I had signed was. He said, it's like this Mr. Sego, if two people get into an accident by one running into another, even though one is clearly at fault, the other has to sue to get justice, there is no contract there. I told him that this is not any accident. When I asked him to provide the implementing regulations for the individual tax statute he told me that he was not going to show me anything more.

I pulled out a copy of 1.1-1 taken from IRC 26, and I asked him if this was the individual tax. He didn't want to answer (but remember the tape recorders were running and I had three witnesses). If he said no, I didn't owe anything, if he said yes, I still didn't owe him anything. He finally said, yes.

I told him that 1.1-1 is only referenced to Form 2555, Foreign earned Income. He couldn't say anything, he was had. I told him that the 1040 was an illegal form and asked him if he was trying to tell me to do something illegal. Just silence. He insisted that I needed to file 1040 forms. I asked him if it was mandatory to file the 1040s.

The agent said yes. I informed him about the head of Alcohol Tobacco and Firearms, under oath in front of Congress, testified that filing was 100 percent voluntary. I then asked the IRS agent, who was lying—him or the Head of Alcohol Tobacco and Firearms. He said neither was lying. After this he got mad and terminated our meeting. I didn't want to leave, but he insisted.

Pretax court:

I started requesting my files from the IRS under the Freedom of Information Act. The IRS had created an account for me showing that all of the money I had earned, originated out of the Virgin Islands. My wife had received a letter before this, telling her that her account had been changed, and now she owed half of what I owed. They of course were trying to get to my family. The very next letter she received, was a notice of intent to levy. They obviously had failed to follow their own procedure, and knowing that the whole thing can be thrown out because of this violation, we were talked into filing an appeal to the tax court.

The Tax Court was held April 10, 2000, but about two days prior, we agreed to meet with the IRS to try and resolve the Tax Court issues as requested by the Tax Court Judge. So we did.

In attendance for the IRS was the Senior Special Investigator of Couer D' Alene, Idaho and IRS Attorney from Seattle, Washington. For our side was, myself and my wife, Davina.

My wife and I went in acting as though we were anxious to cooperate, and as though we wanted to get the issues settled. The way we were received was with great excitement and with relief that we were finally broken down enough to give in. We were actually on a fishing expedition. The agent from Coeur D' Alene admitted that the reason that we were targeted in the first place is that an anonymous caller had pointed us out. He also said that if we hadn't ever owned any land that we would not have been bothered. He showed me every business transaction that I had ever made, and explained how I had made it. He also admitted that I wasn't hiding anything, so therefore, wasn't subject to tax evasion. The IRS attorney stated that if we were serious about wanting to get this situation resolved that we should file 1040 forms to show our intent. The agent from Coeur D' Alene, told me that Davina didn't need to, but I should come down to the IRS office in Coeur d' Alene the following Monday and that I could file 1040s and that somebody would be glad to help me. He said, "Davina you can stay home, is all we need is Steven".

He told me to come to the office on Monday and bring my own envelope, my own stamps and that I was to address the envelope myself, put my own stamps on it, file, sign, drop the forms in the envelope, and seal it myself and then he would accompany me to the post office and watch me drop it in the mail.

He then asked me if I wanted to pay state taxes. I said of course not. He said, well if you do it the way I said, then you won't have to pay state taxes. Davina asked him how that worked. He said, by doing it the way he suggested I could avoid state taxes, and that I could trust him.

As we were getting ready to leave the meeting, I told the IRS that I knew how it justified its' proceeding against me. I say I am sovereign, but because I work for a corporation, the IRS treats my wages as Foreign Earned Income. They both agreed, "That's right."

After we had gone out of the Federal building where the meeting was held, I asked my wife, if she realized that the Coeur D' Alene investigator and the IRS attorney had tried to set me up and send me to prison on two felonies. She was almost sick when she came to the realization.

Tax court:

At tax court on April 10, 2000, we appeared only to contest the deficiency notice to my wife, which she did not receive. The witness for the IRS was a mail lady who supposedly had delivered the notices of certified mail to our mail box. When it was our turn to question the witness, she said that she remembered delivering us the notices back in 1997, but she could not remember the names of the roads that she supposedly drives every day. There were two notices for two certified letters, the first notice was supposedly signed by her, but hadn't any signature or writing at all. The second, she testified, "this is my signature" and the letters were "RIS". Her initials would be L.V., which doesn't match the initials at all.

When we were done questioning the witness, the judge told us that if either of us wanted to say anything that we would have to be sworn in under oath and take the stand. We knew that if we wanted our story out that one of us would have to take the stand and one of us would have to ask the questions. Davina, decided that she would rather take the stand, and so, was sworn in.

I asked her questions and in the process, were able to show how the IRS had fabricated everything to do with the Notice of Deficiency that was supposedly sent. We used things that the IRS Attorney had said in our meeting, prior to the Tax Court, against him. I do not believe the IRS were ready for what they got. After the testifying, the Judge admitted that it was obvious that Davina didn't receive a deficiency notice, but that she would review the evidence and make a ruling later. The ruling later, however, was in favor of the IRS, which of course, was to be expected.

Before the Tax Court had started, I had requested a transcript of the proceedings. When the transcript had finally been sent to us, on review, I noticed that vital information had been omitted from the transcript. The part where the postal witness for the IRS, testified that her signature was on the attempted delivery notices, was missing. I immediately sent for a copy of the tape from the transcribers, located in Stockton, California. They notified me that the written word would serve me better and that they do not keep the tapes, but get rid of them. I have requested the tape another time. I just happened to have two witnesses in the court on that day, to prove the truth, plus I immediately made out affidavits and have sent them to the congressmen and women.

I heard nothing from the IRS until June 18, 2001, when the same IRS agent from Idaho Falls, Idaho and the original agent from Coeur D' Alene, Idaho showed up at my door. I saw them coming and went out to meet them. The agent from Idaho Falls asked, "Are you Mr. Sego?"

I said, "Yes".

He said, we are going to seize your property soon if you don't cooperate. I ordered him to leave before he could say anything more. He stuttered and said, "Okay". They turned around and left. As they were turning, I said, "and don't come back, the only thing you are going to get is a lawsuit slapped against you so fast it won't quit."

They didn't say another word. I believe that the reason they came at that time is because, they thought my wife and family was home, alone, and they intended to intimidate her.

I know that we can prevail, by holding up God's Law and maintaining true principles.

You see, I knew the IRS is a fraud, and I knew that the 1040 Form is a fraudulent form, and now, if I was to file a demand or request for money on a form that I know is fraudulent, and make the demand, like everyone does every year, by mail, then I would have just committed mail fraud. Moreover, the IRS agent would be the star witness, because he would have watched me sign the form, which is affirmation to my intent, and then to top it all off, would witness against me by watching me drop it in the mail box. This would be a sure fire conviction, which would send me up the creek without a paddle for 10 years. Since, at this time, I had not filed for 1993, 1994, and 1995, so if I filed a 1040 for each of these years, like the agents, in that meeting were wanting me to, then that would equal three counts of mail fraud, with a ten-year prison penalty for each, On top of that, if I didn't file state taxes, but I filed only federal, then it would be construed as avoiding, or tax evasion, which is a felony, with the penalty of another 10 years in prison. The total, possible prison time could equal forty (40)-years. I could possibly have been in prison for the rest of my life. The key to follow is this, if you don't owe or file federal taxes, then you don't owe state taxes.

It is now 2020, and I have not filed for almost 30 years. I have not been bothered anymore by the IRS, as I have kept out of their corporate jurisdiction. *"19. If ye were of the world, the world would love his own: but because ye are not of the world, but I have chosen you out of the world, therefore the world hateth you." (John 15:19, KJV)* The editor of the "Idaho Observer" Don Harkins, a great patriot, now deceased, put my story on the internet. Last I heard, my case was being used as a test case by attorneys, trying to figure out what I did. It talks about how Steven and Davina fought the IRS to a standstill.

"6. My people are destroyed for lack of knowledge..." (Hosea 4:6, KJV) God gives knowledge to those who are diligent, with the faith they exercise, in the knowledge they have, and then he gives more knowledge as it is used. When we tell God to take us and use us the way he sees fit, then be ready because faith can really hurt. I thank God every day for the knowledge he has given me, so that I can maybe, inspire others to do his will and understand and find their path back to him. I feel that I have really lived.

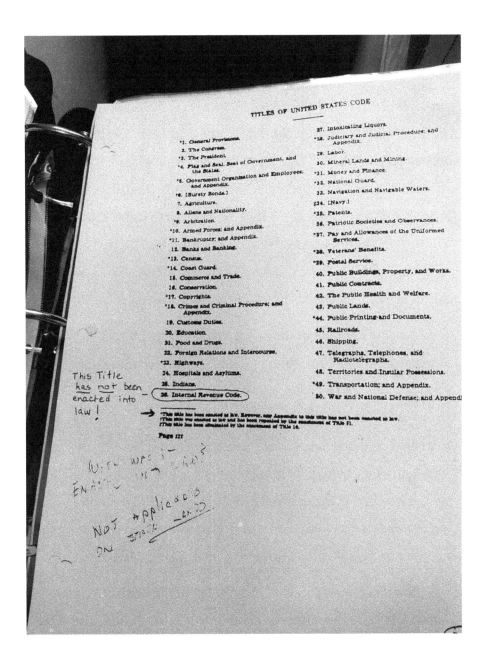

CHAPTER 2
What Kind of Citizen You Are

"24. And when they were come to Capernaum, they that received **tribute money** came to Peter, and said, **Doth not your master pay tribute?**" "25. He saith, yes. And when he was come into the house, Jesus prevented him, saying, what thinkest thou, Simon? **Of whom do the kings of the earth take customs or tribute? Of their own children, or of strangers?**" "26. Peter saith unto him, **Of strangers**. Jesus saith unto him, **Then are the children free.**" (Matthew 17:24-26, KJV)

Ask yourself the question. Are you a "United States" citizen, a stranger from another foreign country, a corporation/corporate person, or, are you a citizen of The America-Republic, or, as Christ put it, a "child of the country"? He was telling Peter, that your immediate country only taxes the foreigner, and not the citizen of the country they belong to. In this case, America. If you are a natural born, sovereign, or naturalized citizen under the Constitution, then you are one of the "children" that Christ is talking about, and you are free by law. Therefore, no custom or tribute is necessary.

Christ just told Peter, that if the kings of the earth only demand "tribute" from the stranger, or in other words, the "foreigner", then the children, or in other words, the "natural born citizen", or "naturalized citizen" is free. Tribute is foreign earned income. Christ understanding now that Peter had opened up a can of worms that might offend those who receive tribute, told Peter to go to the ocean, or sea, which symbolizes a foreign jurisdiction, so that tribute money could be paid to them fairly, and lawfully as foreign earned income. "Notwithstanding, lest we should offend them, go thou to the **sea**, and cast in a hook, and take up the fish that first cometh up; and when thou hast opened his mouth, thou shalt find a piece of money: that take, and give unto them for me and thee." (Matthew 17:27, KJV)

The Pharisees, were always trying to outsmart Christ into doing or saying something that would trip him up, into making it appear, as him breaking the law. Christ however, was too smart for them. "Then went the Pharisees, and took counsel how they might entangle him in his talk. And they sent unto him their disciples with the Herodians, saying, Master, we know that thou art true, and teachest the way of God in truth, neither carest thou for any man: for thou regardest not the person of men. Tell us therefore, What thinkest thou? Is it lawful to **give tribute unto Caesar, or not?** But Jesus perceived their wickedness, and said, Why tempt ye me, ye hypocrites? Shew me the **tribute money**. And they brought unto him a penny. And he sayeth unto them, Whose is this **image and superscription?** They say unto him, Caesar's. Then saith he unto them, **Render therefore unto Caesar the things which are**

Caesar's; and unto God the things that are God's. (Matthew 22:15-22, KJV)

The reader must understand the times that Christ was in. Rome was occupying Israel at this time. They were a foreign nation trying to subject Israel to their way of thinking, by trying to implement their system of government onto the people. That included commerce, and the money system, the laws, etc. Christ understands government and what the implications of tribute are and what it means. He is well aware of the correct words to use to stay out of their jurisdiction. Christ asks them questions, well knowing that they are trying to trick him. He tells them to show him the tribute money used to pay Caesar. Upon seeing the superscription on the penny, he can see that of Caesar, and automatically knows that it is a foreign money as opposed to lawful currency of the country of Israel, and so is immediately able to tell them that it is Caesar's and he wants no part of it, so give it back to Caesar. At the same time he tells them to also give to God those things that are God's. In other words, pay to Caesar that which belongs or is just to Caesar, but don't rob your countrymen to pay Caesar. What you do unto your fellowman, you do unto God.

The governments at the time of Paul were all systems of force, and were different than our system of freedom, here in America. When there was not freedom of the people, the laws were determined by a Liberal king and his councilors, if any.

Today, America stands as the only bastion of Freedom. America is the only country in the world that is "free by law". The "Supreme Law of the Land" is the Constitution. It is a law "Of the People", "By the People", and For the People.

Jesus just told them that if the money belongs to Caesar, then by all means, give it to Caesar, but if it doesn't, then give it to whom it belongs. In America's case, the "fiat" money we use is created by the "private corporation", the Federal Reserve Bank. We are in debt to them as long as we have their IOU's in our pockets. Give their alleged money back to them, and tell them to take a hike. The U.S. Treasury is the only lawful source for creating America's money, under the Constitution, backed by gold and silver. In fact the Federal Reserve System must be stopped.

In our Constitution, it talks of three lawful taxes. They are: import, export, and excise taxes. Import taxes are paid when our government, or its corporations bring into the country products from other countries. Export taxes are paid when we ship products out of our country to other countries. Excise taxes are lawful taxes every American pays on goods and services that they use, such as sales tax on food, when they buy fuel at the pump, when they use the public library, police services, fire fighter services etc. In other words, an excise tax is a tax where if you use something, then you pay for it. These taxes go towards supporting the government, both state and federal. Any taxes other than these are both unlawful and fraudulent, and meant for the control and servitude of the people.

This is what Christ meant, when he said. If the money belongs to government, then give it to the government, but if it doesn't, then give it to whom it belongs. Then can the children of the land be free. You don't rob Peter to pay Paul. (See ten planks of communist manifesto). However, because our U.S. Treasury is not doing what it was intended for, then we as the people are forced to use fake or fraudulent IOU's to carry on in commerce, and find it necessary to gain knowledge of, and exercise our "Remedies" accordingly, and assert our Constitutional Rights. Once again, the Communist Manifesto put into place by evil Democrats, threatens the freedom of America.

The first thing you need to decide is, who you are. Are you a stranger or are you one of the children? If you are one of the children, a naturalized citizen of America, a sovereign, or natural born citizen of America, under the Constitution, with Common Law Jurisdiction, then you are free and do not owe the IRS anything. Anything you make is "Remuneration" and not "Income". If you are a foreigner, or a "person" such as a federal employee, a corporation, etc. then you are the stranger that receives income, and the filing requirement applies to you. (see Black's Law Dictionary, **"Person"** "In general usage, a human being(i.e. Natural person), though **by statute term** may include labor organizations, partnerships, associations, corporations, legal representatives, trustees, trustees in bankruptcy, or receivers. See e.g. National Labor Relations Act~2(1), 29mU.S.C.A.~152; Union Partnership Act.~2. As a federal employee, you should never file a 1040 form, that being fraudulent. You should only file the 2555 form, for the amount of foreign earned income you acquired.

There can be no enforcement of filing requirements on the 1040 form. The form is a fraudulent document on its surface, as it has a false "Office of Management and Budget" (OMB) number, and is also part of the "Paper Reduction Act" both of which makes it a fraudulent document.

When the IRS sends you a "Notice of Levy on Wages, Salary, and Other Incomes", for payment of a tax on a 1040 form, they omit several sections in the Notice which deal with, who is required to file. The IRS is full of lies and deceptions, in order to fool the people into believing they owe some unlawful tax in the first place. So, you need to know who you are before you are lead blindly into believing you owe a tax on your hard earned "Remuneration".

On the "Notice of Levy", you are immediately intimidated by the information it displays. First and foremost, is that it is from the mighty IRS, which is almost a heart stopper on its own, then you see numbers: "1040" tax, the amount of alleged unpaid taxes, the amount of alleged additional amounts, and then the totals, which almost blow you away. The first thing that comes to your mind is; "I don't owe that much".

What you need to remember is that you **don't owe them anything**, and remember who you are. If you are a natural born citizen, or naturalized citizen, and domiciled within one of the several states, then this levy does not apply to you. All of the answers can be found in the information of the IRS, but you need to find it. It is very obvious, and most of the time is like finding a needle in a haystack. Some of it is outright obnoxious, other things are implied, and much of it is knowing what they are not showing you, and then understanding it. In the case of the levy, you are bombarded with lies and intimidation, but it is what they have omitted on the back, where the answer is.

It says "excerpts from the Internal Revenue Code", then goes to "Sec. 6331. Levy and Distraint." It leaves out (a) where it would explain the authority of the Secretary, and goes straight to (b) then (c). It omits (d), which explains Salary and Wages to be levied upon, being they are foreigners or corporate persons.

The levy form then goes through "Sec. 6332. Surrender of Property Subject to Levy". It goes through (a), omits (b), talks about (c)(1) and (2), then (d) and omits (e), which explains "Person" to be levied upon. So I found a handbook of the Internal Revenue Code and looked up Sec. 6331. (a) and it reads, "Levy may be made upon the accrued salary or wages of any officer, employee, or elected official, of the United States, the District of Columbia, or any agency instrumentality of the United States or the District of Columbia, by

TO HELL, WITH THE IRS!

serving a notice of levy on the employer (as defined in section 3401(d) of such officer, employee, or elected official." So unless you are one of these, the IRS has no jurisdiction over you. (See notice of levy).

(See "Compendium of Studies of International Income and Taxes), 1979-1983" page 445). In this literature, the 1040 form is grouped together with nonresidents, nonresident aliens, permanent citizens, U.S citizens, such as those from territories, like Puerto Rico, Guam, American Samoa, Virgin Islands, Corporations, and Foreign Trusts. These are the real corporate "United States of America". The 1040 form is the form for obtaining information individually, from one of the above, thus deceiving the Sovereign citizen. Even then, the 1040 Form is not a lawful document at all, as it displays a fraudulent OMB number. The correct form to be filing for those making "Foreign Earned Income" is the "Form 2555", forgetting the 1040 form altogether.

(See 26 CFR Ch. I (4-1-98 Edition) "...except that the term does not include an individual who is a citizen of Guam but not otherwise a citizen of the United States. An individual who is a citizen of Guam but not otherwise a citizen of the United States is any individual who has become a citizen of the United States by birth or naturalization in Guam". In other words, if you are born in Guam you are a U.S. Citizen. If you move from another country to Guam, and are naturalized there, you are a U.S. Citizen. To be a United States citizen means that you are under the jurisdiction of the federal government and territories, and not under the Constitution, and Common Law Jurisdiction.

Today, all naturalized citizens are presumed to be citizens of the "United States of America", the corporate name for the federal government, and are subject to withholding. However, those lawfully naturalized, and domiciled within one of the several "united states of America" the "Republic", name of a free people, are not subject to withholding. The "naturalized citizen", in order to assert their Common Law Rights under the Constitution, need to know the difference. It makes sense, that the "Naturalized Citizen" is free under the Constitution, as their children will be natural born, and for sure are free. So why not the naturalized citizen?

(See 26 CFR 1.1-2). (b) "Citizens or residents of the United States liable to tax. In general, all citizens of the United States, wherever resident, and all resident alien individuals are liable to the income taxes imposed by the Code whether the income is received from sources within or without the United States. Pursuant to section 876, a nonresident alien individual who is a bona fide resident of Puerto Rico during the entire taxable year is, except as provided in section 933 with respect to Puerto Rican source income, subject to taxation in the same manner as a resident alien individual".

So, if you are born in Puerto Rico, you are a citizen of the United States. If you come from somewhere else and are just living in Puerto Rico, then you are a resident of the United States, and both are subject to the individual income tax. You see, the money you make is considered as foreign earned income, from a foreign source. "Income" means, incoming revenue from a foreign source, completely in sync with the meaning of the 16th Amendment, which states: "The Congress shall have power to lay and collect taxes on incomes, from whatever source derived, without apportionment among the several States, and without regard to any census or enumeration."

By incorporating your business, or church, or simply working for a corporation can be a source of foreign earned income, whether you are in Guam, or Puerto Rico, Washington D.C. etc., or in the several states. However, if it is "Remuneration" you earn from a corporation, located in America-Republic, and as long as you are a natural-born, or naturalized citizen, domiciled within one of the several states, then it cannot be construed as "Income".

There are two separate countries that no one bothers to teach you about. One is the corporate United States, which includes the District of Columbia, all of the territories, any and all enclaves of jurisdiction of the United States, within the boundaries of the States, such as post offices, armed forts, ships, military bases, corporations, immigration, etc., these are under the Admiralty jurisdiction. If you are a citizen of one of the several United States of America, which includes businesses and churches who are unincorporated, then you are under the Constitution and Common Law Jurisdiction, and the IRS does not apply to you.

Taken from the Code of Federal Regulations of Title 26, Internal Revenue Code~1.1-1, revised as of April 1, 1998: "Normal Taxes and Surtaxes" "Determination of Tax Liability" "Tax on Individuals" ~ "**1.1-1** Income tax on Individuals" "(a) General rule. (1) Section 1 of the Code imposes an income tax on the income of every individual who is a citizen or resident of the **United States** and, to the extent provided by section 871(b) or 877(b), on the income of **nonresident alien individual....**" So you see, a resident of the United States is someone who is not from the United States but living there, otherwise a foreigner. A citizen of the United States is someone born into a territory or corporation of the United States. That means that a citizen from one of the several united states, a sovereign citizen under the Constitution, but not invoking the proper jurisdiction under the Constitution, can be regarded as a resident of the United States, therefore out of ignorance is coerced into servitude of the corporate system, and made to believe he/she is liable to the income tax.

1.1-2, Title 26 CFR, Internal Revenue Code. "(b) Citizens or residents of the United States liable to tax. In general, all citizens of the United States, wherever resident, and all resident alien individuals are liable to the income taxes imposed by the code whether the income is received from sources within or without the

United States..." "(c) who is a citizen. Every person born or naturalized in the United States and subject to its jurisdiction is a citizen...." You can see here that all persons or individuals are all grouped together with those as residents, non-residents, non-resident aliens etc. and the jurisdiction allotted to them is admiralty jurisdiction, which is a jurisdiction of force, and the way it is maintained is by threat, duress and coercion.

26 CFR **1.911-2**"Qualified Individuals" "(a) In general. An individual is a qualified individual if: (1) The individuals tax home is in a foreign country or countries throughout---..." So, to be a qualified individual you simply need to be a foreigner. What the IRS doesn't tell you, is that they consider a foreigner of the United States, to be, merely a sovereign citizen of a state Republic, and working for a corporation, therefore the source of income is considered as foreign earned income.

"The laws of Congress in respect to those matters(outside of Constitutionally delegated powers) do not extend into the territorial limits of the states, but have **force ONLY in the District of Columbia**, and other places that are within the **exclusive jurisdiction** of the national government." Caha V. US, 152 U.S. 211. "Special provision is made in the Constitution for the cession of jurisdiction from the states over places where the federal government shall establish forts or other military works. And is only in these places, or in territories of the United States, where it can exercise a general jurisdiction". New Orleans V. US, 35 US (10 Pet.) 662 (1836) Supreme Court. "Constitutional restrictions and limitations were not applicable to the areas of lands, enclaves, territories and possessions over which Congress had exclusive legislative authority". Downs V. Bidwell, 132 US 244. **It is a well-established principle of law that all federal legislation applies only within the territorial jurisdiction of the United States unless a contrary intent appears."** Foley Brothers, Inc. V. Filardo, 336 US 281 (1948).

Before an administrative agency can move, they first must prove they have jurisdiction. "Jurisdiction is essential to give validity to the determinations of administrative agencies and where jurisdictional requirements are not satisfied, the action of the agency is a nullity..." City Street Improv. Co. V. Pearson, 181 C 640, 185 P. 962; O'Neil V. Dept. of Professional & Vocational Standards, 7 CA2d 393, 46 P2d 234. "The law requires PROOF of jurisdiction to appear on the record of the administrative agency and all administrative proceedings." Hagans V. Lavine, 415 US 533.

The 1st through the 13th Articles of the Constitution were placed and worded in the "Bill of Rights" by "We the People, Of the People, and For the People," whereas the rest were placed there by the federal government, for the federal government. That means that the 16th Amendment is by the federal government, for the federal government, and does not apply to the natural born, sovereign citizen under the Constitution. See Federal Rules of Criminal Procedure, Rule 54, (5)(c), "Application of terms." "As used in these rules the following terms have the designated meanings." "**Act of Congress**". Includes **any act of Congress** locally applicable to and in force in the District of Columbia, in Puerto Rico, in a territory or in an insular possession." **"Magistrate Judge"** includes a United States magistrate judge as defined in 28 U.S.C.~631-639, a judge of the United States, another judge or judicial officer specifically empowered by statute in force in any territory or possession, the commonwealth of Puerto Rico, or the District of Columbia, to perform a function to which a particular rule relates, and a **state** or local judicial officer, authorized by 18 U.S.C.~3041 to perform the functions prescribed in Rules 3, 4, and 5." **"State"** includes District of Columbia, Puerto Rico, territory and insular possession."

So the United States of America is the name of the Federal Corporation, and only has jurisdiction in the District of Columbia, Puerto Rico, territories and other insular possessions, whereas the several United States of America is the name of the "Republic" that we talk about every time we say the "pledge of allegiance". So you see, there are really two different countries that are always striving for jurisdiction, even as God strives against the Devil.

What country do you belong to? We are told by the scriptures to be in the world, but not joined to it. The IRS represents the world, and brings with it "chains of hell". The Federal United States represents the first corporation, and is the seat of the devil, as Satan is a system of force, whereas the several United States of America represents freedom under the Constitution, and is the "Supreme Law of the Land", and is the seat of Jesus Christ.

The best way to get confirmation of facts are to go to different sources to see if they have the same meanings, and say the same thing. Let's go to Black's Law Dictionary and look up both definitions of [state]. Black's Law Dictionary, 5th Edition, **"state"** "A people permanently occupying a fixed territory bound together by common-law habits and custom into one body politic exercising, through the medium of an organized government. Independent sovereignty and control over all persons and things within its boundaries, capable of making war and peace and of entering into international relations with other communities of the globe. United States v. Kusche..." This is a "Republic".

The Internal Revenue Service understand their jurisdiction well, but the sheeple don't understand it, therefore, it is easy to deceive them because they won't seek knowledge. Title 26 of the Internal Revenue Code, 3121(1) **"State"** "The term "State" includes the District of Columbia, the Commonwealth of Puerto Rico, the Virgin Islands, Guam, and American Samoa." (2) **"United States"** "The term "United States" when used in a geographical sense includes the Commonwealth of Puerto Rico, the Virgin Islands, Guam, and American Samoa." "An individual who is a citizen of the

Commonwealth of Puerto Rico (but not otherwise a citizen of the United States) shall be considered for purposes of this section, as a citizen of the United States." This is a "Democracy".

So, what this chapter all boils down to is, that there is a corporate or federal country under the corporate name of "The United States of America", and then there is a Sovereign Republic of the "several united states of America". Each of these have very different jurisdictions, and to our Republic under Common Law Jurisdiction, the IRS cannot come unless invited. It is up to each Individual to gain knowledge and either give in or tell them to take a hike. What the states appeared to have ratified as the 16th Amendment back in 1913, was in essence, with no effect on a natural born citizen, or naturalized citizen under the Constitution. It is all in the wording, and the understanding, and jurisdiction.

Bill Benson wrote the book, "The Law That Never Was". In this book he gathered information from every state and showed that not one state ratified the 16th Amendment. However, even if they did ratify it, it doesn't apply to a sovereign citizen, or natural born citizen, or naturalized citizen under the Constitution of the Republic of America. It applies only to Immigration, foreigners, aliens, residents, corporations, etc…

If you visit the website of the: Office of the "Law Revision Counsel of the United States House of Representatives", you will find listed all of the United States Codes. Many will have before the number of the code, an Asterisk * symbol. If you look closely, you will see that title 26 does not have an asterisk by it. It is explained: "The United States Code is a consolidation and codification by subject matter of the **general and permanent** laws of the United States. It is prepared by the Office of the Law Revision Counsel of the United States House of Representatives." At the Bottom the * is explained. "*This title has been enacted as **positive law.** However, any appendix to this title has not been enacted as part of the title." Only titles with asterisks have been enacted as positive law. Title 26 is **NOT** positive law, but only "Prima facia", or "colorable law".

I had a meeting called with me, by the U.S. Marshall's office in Coeur D' Alene, Idaho. Denny, in asking me for this meeting, told me to choose the place that we could meet. I chose a little restaurant in down town Rathdrum, called Granny's Pantry. He told me he would be bringing an individual named, Will, representing the FBI. In that meeting we discussed several things, but I remember telling him how jurisdiction worked, and that in our country there are actually two different countries, each with a different jurisdiction. They agreed with me, wholeheartedly, as that is the way it is, no doubt. So just remember who you are, and what country you want to belong to, and resist the one you don't belong to. You can still respect your federal government, but it is the things you say, the things you do, and the knowledge you have that gives jurisdiction. Don't be afraid to do right, and God will bless you with great knowledge.

The Pledge of Allegiance:

"I pledge allegiance to the flag of the United States of America, and to the **Republic**, for which it <u>stands,</u> one Nation under **God**, indivisible, with liberty and justice for all."

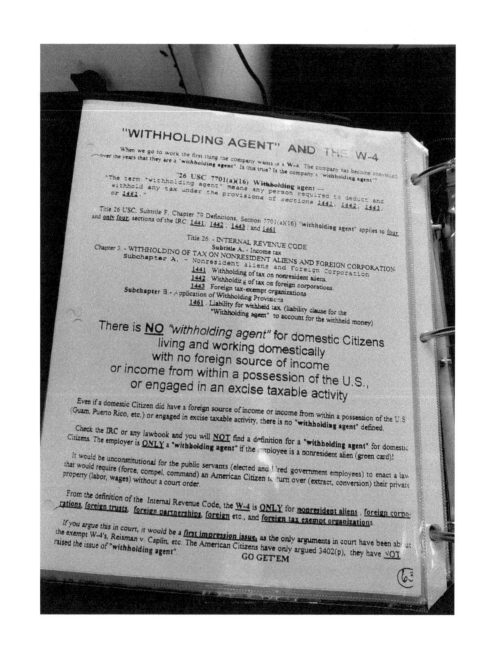

"WITHHOLDING AGENT" AND THE W-4

When we go to work the first thing the company wants is a W-4. The company has become convinced over the years that they are a "withholding agent". Is this true? Is the company a "withholding agent"?

"26 USC 7701(a)(16) **Withholding agent**.—
"The term "withholding agent" means any person required to deduct and withhold any tax under the provisions of sections 1441, 1442, 1443, or 1461."

Title 26 USC, Subtitle F, Chapter 79 Definitions, Section 7701(a)(16) "withholding agent" applies to <u>four</u> and <u>only four</u>, sections of the IRC: <u>1441</u>; <u>1442</u>; <u>1443</u>; and <u>1461</u>

Title 26. - INTERNAL REVENUE CODE
Subtitle A. - Income tax
Chapter 3. - WITHHOLDING OF TAX ON NONRESIDENT ALIENS AND FOREIGN CORPORATION
Subchapter A. - Nonresident aliens and Foreign Corporation
1441. Withholding of tax on nonresident aliens.
1442. Withholding of tax on foreign corporations.
1443. Foreign tax-exempt organizations
Subchapter B. - Application of Withholding Provisions
1461. Liability for withheld tax. (liability clause for the "Withholding agent" to account for the withheld money)

There is **NO** "withholding agent" for domestic Citizens living and working domestically with no foreign source of income or income from within a possession of the U.S., or engaged in an excise taxable activity

Even if a domestic Citizen did have a foreign source of income or income from within a possession of the U.S. (Guam, Puerto Rico, etc.) or engaged in excise taxable activity, there is no "**withholding agent**" defined.

Check the IRC or any lawbook and you will **NOT** find a definition for a "**withholding agent**" for domestic Citizens. The employer is **ONLY** a "**withholding agent**" if the employee is a nonresident alien (green card)!

It would be unconstitutional for the public servants (elected and hired government employees) to enact a law that would require (force, compel, command) an American Citizen to turn over (extract, conversion) their private property (labor, wages) without a court order.

From the definition of the Internal Revenue Code, the <u>W-4</u> is **ONLY** for <u>nonresident aliens</u>, <u>foreign corporations</u>, <u>foreign trusts</u>, <u>foreign partnerships</u>, <u>foreign</u> etc., and <u>foreign tax exempt organizations</u>.

If you argue this in court, it would be a <u>first impression issue</u>, as the only arguments in court have been about the exempt W-4's, Reisman v. Caplin, etc. The American Citizens have only argued 3402(p), they have <u>NOT</u> raised the issue of "**withholding agent**".

GO GET'EM

CHAPTER 3
No Implementing Regulations/No Force of Law

Any time a law is enacted by Congress, "Implementing Regulations" must be put into place to make the law enacted, have force of law. Without these implementing regulations, it is the same as not having any law at all. In the case of the 16th Amendment, or Title 26 USC, this is the case. There are no implementing regulations to enforce the "federal income tax." It is only by threat, duress, and coercion, and through the lies and deception of the IRS, that they have the success that they have had. In all reality, the IRS is a band of corporate robbers, working among themselves, and for the Federal Reserve Bank, in fleecing the people.

United States V. Mersky, 361 US 431, IL ed 2d 423, 80 S Ct 459, "Once promulgated, these regulations, called for by the statute itself, have the force of law, and violations thereof incur criminal prosecutions, just as if all the details had been incorporated into the congressional language. The result is that neither the statute nor the regulations are complete without the other, and only together do they have any force. In effect, therefore, the construction of one necessarily involves the construction of the other."

There are no Title 26 CFR enforcement regulations, meaning that a criminal action under Title 26 USC would be a "colorable" cause of action. This means that it would be brought under false and fraudulent, and malicious prosecution by the government and the court. Everything associated with Title 26 CFR is referenced in the implementing regulations associated with Title 27 CFR, which is to do with alcohol, tobacco and firearms. What has the individual income tax got to do with alcohol, tobacco, and firearms? The answer is nothing, except it is used to be scary and deceptive to the ignorant individual. (See table-Internal Revenue Service Authority for Assessment. Lien, Summons, etc.).

On Page 564 of 37 Federal Rules Decisions, United States of America, Libellant v. $3,976.62 IN CURRENCY, One 1960 Ford Station Wagon Serial No. 0C66W145329. United States District Court, S.D. New York, March 22, 1965, "...1. Federal Civil Procedure~31".

"Although, presumably for the purpose of obtaining **jurisdiction**, action for forfeiture under Internal Revenue Laws is commenced as proceeding in **admiralty.** After jurisdiction is obtained, proceeding takes on character of civil action at law ..."

This means that the IRS comes in and scares the people by intimidation, through threat, duress, and coercion, into getting the people to agreeing, to give up their property: land, automobiles, remuneration [money], etc... This is their part of admiralty jurisdiction. Once they scare the people bad enough for them to voluntarily give information in the favor of the IRS, now the IRS can continue in a civil case. What this means, is that the IRS gets the people to voluntarily waive their Constitutional rights, mainly the 5th Amendment, by witnessing against themselves ignorantly.

They only need two witnesses to proceed in an action at law. They witness against you, and if you volunteer information, that you shouldn't have, then you have just witnessed against yourself, making it the second witness. Now they can file a criminal complaint with the proper authorities, because they have no police power in, and of themselves. Therefore, you never admit you owe the IRS anything, if you are a sovereign citizen, under the Constitution within the jurisdiction of a state boundary. You always say, I owe you nothing.

The money you make is always "Remuneration" and not "Income" as from a foreign country. You are always a sovereign citizen, and natural born or naturalized under the Constitution and its Common Law Jurisdiction. You never say you are a citizen of the United States when dealing with the IRS. You are always a citizen of the several united states of America-Republic. Jurisdiction means everything. Don't ever enter into any deal with them. Instead go down their throats and treat them like the robbers they are.

A Richard Durjak, wrote a letter to the Director of the Federal Register and asked him if there were any sections under Title 26 of the Code of Federal Regulations with implementing regulations. A Michael I. White responded saying: "...The Parallel Table of

Authorities and Rules, a finding aid compiled and published by the Office of the Federal Register (OFR) as a part of the CFR Index, indicates that implementing regulations for the sections cited above have been published in various parts of title 27 of the Code of Federal Regulations (CFR). There are no corresponding entries for title 26." He goes on to add: "Our records indicate that the Internal Revenue Service has not incorporated by reference in the Federal Register (as that term is defined in the Federal Register system) a requirement to make an income tax return."

A Pat Danner of the House of Representatives, Congressman from Missouri, wrote to a Bill Petterson with these words, dated September 12, 1996: "You are quite correct when you state that an organization with the actual name "Internal Revenue Service" was not established by law. Instead, in 1862, Congress approved 26 U.S.C. 7802. This statute established the office of "Commissioner of Internal Revenue." As the act states, "The Commissioner of Internal Revenue" shall have such duties and powers as may be prescribed by the "Secretary of the Treasury." In modern times these duties and powers flow to the Commissioner who implements appropriate policy through the IRS." (See letter dated September 12, 1996, from Pat Danner).

"Policy" here, is the key word. Policy and procedure does not carry the force of law, pertaining to the citizen under the Constitution of the several United States of America. If that were so, then every business who makes policy for their businesses, would be in the business of making law. The Internal Revenue laws are only applicable to foreigners of the United States of America, while in the United States, within Admiralty Jurisdiction.

In an "Internal Revenue Service/ Internal Revenue Code Investigative Report" by William Cooper. He uncovered many irregularities of the IRS. Here are just some of the things that were exposed: "...What we uncovered has clearly been designed to circumvent the limitations of the Constitution for the United States of America and implement the Communist Manifesto within the 50 States. Marx and Engles claimed that in the effort to create a classless society, a "**graduated income tax**" could be used as a weapon to destroy the middle class."

"Not Created by Congress" "The Bureau of Internal/Revenue, and the alleged Internal /Revenue Service were not created by Congress. These are not organizations or agencies of the Department of Treasury or of the federal government. They appear to be operated through pure trusts administered by the Secretary of the Treasury (the Trustee). The Settler [Settlor] of the trusts and the Beneficiary or Beneficiaries are unknown. According to the law governing trusts the information does not have to be revealed."

"Found in 31 USC" "The organization of the Department of the Treasury can be found in 31 United States Code, Chapter 3, beginning on page 7. You will not find the Bureau of Internal

Revenue, the Internal Revenue Service, the Secret Service, or the Bureau of Alcohol, Tobacco and Firearms listed. We learned that the Bureau of Internal Revenue, Internal Revenue, internal revenue, Internal Revenue Service, the Federal Alcohol Administration, Director of Alcohol, Tobacco and Firearms **are one organization**. We found this obfuscated."

"Constructive Fraud" "The investigation found, that except for the very few who are engaged in specific activities, the **Citizens of the 50 States of the United States of America** have **never been required to file or pay "Income taxes."** The federal government is engaged in **constructive fraud** on a massive scale. Americans who have been frightened into filing and paying "income taxes", have been robbed of their money. Millions of lives have been ruined. Hundreds of thousands of innocent people have been imprisoned on the pretense they violated laws that do not exist. Some have been driven to suicide. Marriages have been destroyed. Property has been confiscated to pay... [end of sentence obscured]."

"No Jurisdiction!" "The Bureau of Alcohol, Tobacco, and Firearms has no venue or jurisdiction within the borders of any of the 50 states of the United States of America except in pursuit of an importer of contraband, alcohol, tobacco, or firearms who failed to pay the tax on those items. As proof refer to the July 30, 1993 ruling of the United States Court of appeals for the Seventh Circuit, in F 3d 1511; 1993 U.S. App. Lexis 19747, where the court ruled in

United States v. D.J. Vollmer & Co. that the BATF has jurisdiction over the first sale of a firearm imported to the country but they don't have jurisdiction over subsequent sales." (See investigative report)

I would love nothing more than to see the IRS go out of business, and shut down. That will only happen though, when we the people, armed with knowledge, can expel all Democrats and left leaning Republicans from our government.

CHAPTER 4
Voluntary Compliance System

"HANDBOOK FOR SPECIAL AGENTS" Criminal Investigation Intelligence Division, Internal Revenue Service" "AGENTS...Our tax system is based on **individual self-assessment and voluntary compliance**...the material contained in this handbook is confidential in character...and must not under any circumstances be made available to persons outside the service." "MR. MORTIMER CAPLIN, INTERNAL REVENUE SERVICE, COMMISSIONER."

There you have it right out of the Commissioner's mouth that the income tax system is a voluntary compliance system. The IRS is very well aware that you have Constitutional Rights. From this same handbook for special agents, they discuss how records can be gotten from the individual. For instance, page 9781-89, (7) "The original records of an individual defendant, in his/her possession, cannot be subpoenaed into court for use against him/her in a criminal trial, because to do so would violate his/her constitutional rights against self-incrimination and render his/her records inadmissible. However, authenticated copies of such records are admissible in criminal proceedings."

This means that instead of having a prospective defendant

willingly give records over, the IRS will go to the employer or other sources, and force them to cough up your records. Further, (8)"When records are obtained from a possible defendant, notation should be made of the circumstances to show that they were furnished **voluntarily."** To invoke your Constitutional rights must be done early, and is all you have to say to invoke them is: "I plead the 5th Amendment", or, 4th Amendment, etc... To simply say you are under the Constitution does not assert your rights as well, because it is more vague, and fails to convey the message that you know what you are talking about.

"Internal Revenue Investigation" Hearings before a Subcommittee of the Committee on Ways and Means, House of Representatives, Eighty-Third Congress, First Session on Administration of the Internal Revenue Laws, Part A, Testimony of Dwight E. Avis, head of Alcohol, Tobacco Tax Division, Bureau of Internal Revenue..." "Mr. Avis: There is just no such thing. That is where this structure differs." Let me point this out now: Your income tax is **100 percent voluntary tax**, and your liquor tax is 100 percent enforced tax. Now, the situation is as different as day and night. Consequently, your same rules just will not apply, and therefore the alcohol and tobacco tax has been handled here in this reorganization a little differently, because of the very nature of it, than the rest of the over-all tax problem."

"Estimates of Income Unreported on Individual Income Tax

Returns" Department of the Treasury Internal/Revenue Service, Publication 1104(9-79)", iii third paragraph "...Our objective will be to increase **voluntary compliance** so that the Service's limited resources can be focused on the remaining instances of noncompliance." iv. Second paragraph, "This report confirms that **voluntary reporting of income** is very high where incomes are subject to withholding," Really? Do they call having the company where you work at, acting as a withholding agent, automatically withholding money from someone's paycheck, who just happens to be ignorant, voluntary? Seventh paragraph, "I think **voluntary compliance** turns to a significant but immeasurable extent on the perception and reality that the system treats taxpayers decently and fairly."

Yeah right, but we have established the fact that the IRS wants you to believe that the income tax system is a system of voluntary compliance. What they mean as "voluntary compliance", is that you voluntarily go down to any library, post office or courthouse and pick up your 1040 tax form. Then you fill it out voluntarily, sign it voluntarily, put your own stamp on your own envelope, then voluntarily go down to the post office yourself and drop it in. The IRS wants you to voluntarily commit **mail fraud** on your own. They don't send you the fraudulent form through the mail, otherwise they would be committing the mail fraud. As long as you are doing what they want you to do, through their threat, duress and coercion, then they call that voluntary compliance. To do all of this voluntarily, then is a waiver of your rights, which makes it much easier for them to come after you if you get out of line. Well then, I volunteer not to comply, seeing as I am not a taxpayer, or a resident of the District of Columbia, nor am I a non-resident alien, or a foreigner except to the jurisdiction of the United States. I am a sovereign citizen of the several United States of America, under the Constitution, and it's Common Law Jurisdiction. I refuse to be lied to, and robbed, and I refuse the jurisdiction of a communist system of government, under the Ten Planks of the Communist Manifesto.

As long as the people are ignorant to the facts that the IRS is making fools out of them, and scaring them into giving up their hard earned "remuneration" voluntarily, they are going to continue robbing them of their labor and resources.

Most Occupations out there are "occupations of common right". These such occupations cannot be taxed as a matter of principle, but the people thinking they are getting a benefit at the end of the year by filing their "tax returns", don't stop to realize that there is no tax on an occupation of Common Right. They also don't realize that the IRS is not going to give the people anything, but only a small portion of all the money that they paid into the system for the whole year. This is to make them believe the IRS is being good to them and rewarding them for filing their 1040, thus committing their mail-fraud, and at the same time, not alarming the people.

Harry Reid, a Democratic Senator, replied to a Peter Tolotti: "I consulted the legal and tax divisions of the Congressional Research Service to answer your question. They found no tax on an "Occupation of Common Right."

When you go to work for the first time with a company, they want you to fill out a W-4 form for deducting money from your paychecks on behalf of the IRS. The company has somehow been convinced that they are "withholding agents" for the IRS. Title 26 USC 7701(a)(16) defines withholding agent—"The term "withholding agent" means any person required to deduct and withhold any tax under the provisions of sections **1441, 1442, 1443, or 1461.**" Title 26 USC, subtitle F, Chapter 79 definitions, Section 7701(a)(16) **"withholding agent"** applies to only four sections of the Internal Revenue Code: 1441, 1442, 1443, and 1461.; "Title 26~Internal Revenue Code, Subtitle A. ~Income Tax, chapter 3~subchapter—A." Withholding of tax on Nonresident Aliens and Foreign Corporations", is in 1441; Withholding tax on nonresident aliens, is in 1442; Withholding tax on foreign corporations, is in1443; and foreign tax-exempt organizations; and Subchapter B.-- Application of withholding provisions, is in 1461. Liability for withheld tax. (Liability clause for the "withholding agent" to account for the withheld money).

This is then a pretty cut and dried situation, and to fix it, is all one needs to do is ask your company for another W-4 form, and follow the instructions from chapter 1 of this book, and never file again. I can almost guarantee that anyone working for your company in management positions, is not a withholding agent for the IRS, and they have no authority of doing so. There is NO "withholding agent" for domestic citizens living and working domestically within their respective states, with any foreign source of incoming money, or income from within a possession of the United States, or engaged in any excise taxable activity.

Interesting facts about the incorporated "United States of America" are dated back to the presidential terms that the then, President Ulysses S. Grant, served in the wake of the Civil War. When he took office in 1969, as the 18th president. His term began under the jurisdiction of Common-law, under the Constitution of the several united states of America-Republic. However, he was not to savvy on running a country, or politics, and was easily persuaded by friends and family, and many self interest groups into signing acts to do with disenfranchising our federal government from the people.

In 1871 he signed a document which incorporated Washington D.C., called the "Act of 1871", also known as the "Second Force Act", or the "District of Columbia Organic Act of 1871". Basically, what this Act did was to allow all fiduciary officers, including congress, men and women, senators, presidents, judges etc., in the now incorporated "United States of America", to not be held accountable for their actions. This allowed them to be able to lie, deceive, commit fraud, embezzle, even kill, and not have to answer for their crimes, because Washington D.C. was now a foreign country, as to the several united states of America-Republic. In this manner, they could push any unlawful agency onto the American people, such as the Federal Reserve Bank, and it's muscleman, the IRS, and the people could do nothing about it, because through these agencies, congress, presidents, the senate, judges, etc., all covered each other's backs through the medium of "secret orders" such as the illuminati, Jesuits, and many other secret orders, and got wealthy doing it. They call this prejudicial treatment as "special privileged". President Grant served two terms, from 1869-1877.

In 1938, under "Erie v. Tompkins", a Supreme Court case, became a precedent for disposing of our Common Law under the Constitution, and replacing it with Uniform Commercial Code, under Maritime Law, which all of the courts use today. Even though the Constitution is still the Supreme Law of the land, the individual now is barred from entering a court or tribunal court and arguing Constitutional principles, but all arguments must be done by statute. This is why all states have respective statute law. In Idaho there is Idaho Code, Wisconsin has Wisconsin Code etc. This case of Erie v. Tompkins, must be repealed.

As the churches, have incorporated under the 501(c)(3) charters, and by doing so have become state-run churches. What would be of more service to the people and the cause of liberty, is for these incorporated churches to withdraw their incorporated status. The same thing applies to the incorporated United States of America. By repealing the Second Force Act, or the District of Columbia Organic Act of 1871, would make all elected officials in Washington D.C. accountable to we the people, and give the people back control of their country, and once again make government, of the people, by the people, and for the people, servants of the people.

This is what President Trump meant when he said, he was giving America back to the people. He said, he would never stop fighting, he will never back down, and he will never concede, because he won the 2020 election by a landslide, but the evil Democrats, and GOP Republican traitors, who were compromised, and guilty of collusion and sedition, were desperate to stop him from doing what he had set out to do. They conspired together and appeared to have stolen the election through obvious fraud. They organized their efforts in an all-out attempt to bring America to its knees. However, it will not happen, because it appears that President Trump had already unincorporated Washington D.C... Before he left Washington for what it seems, as the last time. He said that he will be back in some form or another, and the best is yet to come. It is pretty obvious that Joe Biden, has no authority, and for the time being, the military is in control, and the real president of the several united states of America-Republic, is still the lawfully elected, President Donald John Trump, of the people, by the people, and for the people. He is lawfully the 19th President of our Republic, as Joe Biden is an actor on appearance only, and is illegitimate. Consequently, all presidents since Ulysses S. Grant up to Donald Trump, were foreign presidents, and not for the people, but have attempted in making slaves out of the people in the several United States. I am continually praying for President Trump, and for his protection, and welfare. He is a good man, as was George Washington. President Trump will be back after Washington D.C. is cleaned out of the so many traitorous criminals, and we all know who they are.

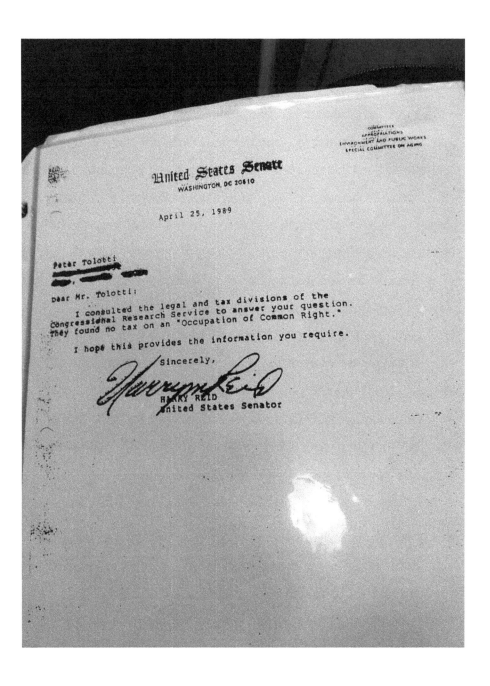

COMMITTEES
APPROPRIATIONS
ENVIRONMENT AND PUBLIC WORKS
SPECIAL COMMITTEE ON AGING

United States Senate
WASHINGTON, DC 20510

April 25, 1989

Peter Tolotti

Dear Mr. Tolotti:

I consulted the legal and tax divisions of the Congressional Research Service to answer your question. They found no tax on an "Occupation of Common Right."

I hope this provides the information you require.

Sincerely,

HARRY REID
United States Senator

CHAPTER 5
The 1040 Form

At the end of every tax season, which is around April of each year, the IRS furnishes forms, which are not mailed to the "individuals" or "persons", but are delivered to every library, post office, or court house, for every individual or person to voluntarily go, get themselves, fill them out, and then mail them in to the IRS. The bulk of the forms are generally the 1040 forms, and then any other form to be attached to the 1040 form, if any, such as the "foreign earned income" form, etc.. The 1040 is the building block for collecting information from these "persons" or "individuals". As long as you are voluntarily complying to their wishes, then not only are you basically waiving your rights under the Constitution, but you are giving them grounds to control you through blackmail. The IRS now feel that they have the jurisdiction to threaten, coerce, and intimidate you from year to year. They have now labeled you as one of their "tax payers", and that you have an "account" with them.

What they are really keeping secret, is that anyone who is a "natural born", or naturalized citizen under the Constitution, is not this kind of individual or person that they have jurisdiction over. Every year though, millions send in their 1040 forms all filled out, expecting to get money back at the end of the year. What they don't realize is that the form they are filing is a fraudulent record, on which they are demanding a benefit, from whom they deem to be a government agency. Ironic, isn't it?

The 1040 form, however is that fraudulent record that they are filing, as it does not display a valid "OMB" number on it. As taken from the instructions for filling out the 2555 form: "Instructions for Form 2555" "foreign earned income" page 4, it states: "*You are not required to provide information requested on a form that is subject to the Paper Reduction Act unless the form displays a valid OMB control number.*" The 1040 form is part of the Paper Reduction Act, and does not display a valid OMB number. The truth is written in their literature somewhere, but you have got to find it and understand it.

The IRS is attempting to collect a tax on all of those "citizens" who are described under Title 26 as citizens under "1.1-1". 1.1-2 defines the type of citizen liable to tax, as talking about the corporate "United States" and not the several "United States". There is a huge difference.

For supposedly collecting a tax on persons or individuals under Title 26 IRC, 1.1-1, the 1040 form displays the OMB number of **1545-0074** (see 1040 form), referencing "alcohol, tobacco and firearms". The form "foreign earned income" form 2555 displays the OMB number **1545-0067.** This number: 1545-0067 is in reference to foreign earned income, form 2555, being the correct number for collecting information from an "individual" or "person".

It is described in title 26: 1.1-2, or citizen or resident of the District of Columbia, Puerto Rico or any other "state" or corporation of the "United States" corporation.

Here is the deceit the IRS uses to fool the people. The income tax they are wanting you to believe you owe is under title 26: 1.1-1, which is referenced to "Foreign Earned Income". The "OMB" number on the 1040 Form, however is referenced to "alcohol, tobacco, and firearms", and only has implementing regulations under Title 27. The common citizen is not liable for either, unless the citizen is of the federal "United States", or is in the occupation of buying and selling alcohol, tobacco, or firearms.

Any "Implementing Regulations" for Title 26 of any returns filed with the IRS are found in Title 27, which is all to do with collecting information on those involved in trafficking alcohol, tobacco and firearms. For instance: Title 26 U.S.C. 6201 assessment authority. Where are the implementing regulations found? In Title 27 U.S.C. 70.71. What about Title 26 U.S.C. 6321 lien for taxes. Where are the implementing regulations? Answer: Title 27 USC 70.141. How about 26 USC 6331; Levy and Distraint? Regulations? Answer: 27 USC 70.161, 162. Are you getting the idea now that the American people have been duped and are acting like just a bunch of sheep? There are no Title 26 CFR enforcement regulations, and the 1040 form is a fraudulent form.

Any criminal action invoked by the IRS under Title 26 CFR

would be a "colorable action", and an abuse of process by the U.S. Attorney. Unless someone within the IRS completes an IRS Form 5546 to indicate that the "taxpayer" is involved in the business of Alcohol, Tobacco, or Firearms, otherwise, this information, of the "individual" or "person" being involved in alcohol, tobacco, or firearms, has been added without his/her knowing, and is "Prima Facia truth unless rebutted by the "taxpayer". So it is very important for you to have a knowledge of who you are first.

CHAPTER 6
No Police Powers

The Internal Revenue Service has made it very hard for just a normal onlooker to catch on to what is, and has really happened. This system is a liberal agency, and have interwoven lie after lie into their literature, and have moved this or that around to deceive and subject the sheeple into believing they are someone they are not, a "taxpayer", and into believing they have an "account", when they do not. Black's Law Dictionary, 6th Edition, **"Account:** *A detailed statement of the mutual demands in the nature of debit and credit between parties, arising out of* **contracts** *or some fiduciary relation"... "a record or course of business dealings between parties;..."*

Every citizen, whether "natural born", or "naturalized" is grouped together with all other "residents" or "aliens", corporations or trusts, etc., and is assumed to be a "corporate" citizen. To be a corporate citizen is an assumption by the corporations/federal government, that all of these minions have no rights and are "DEAD". This is where the term "Straw Man" is derived from. You will frequently see corporations write your name in all capital letters. Most Companies have their computers set up to type your name in all capital letters. In fact, your certified birth certificate issued by your state has written your name all in capital letters. Whereas, your name is to be written in all capital letters on your death certificate after you die. Satan has a "Book of the Dead", whereas, Christ has what is called "The Book of Life".

The IRS does the same thing, and this is why: to assume that the people have no rights, and that they all are "taxpayers" with an account. The account they have, comes from the person filing their 1040 as if they have an incoming supply of revenue from a "foreign source". To pull this one off, the IRS manufactures an account for you, and then codifies it so that you cannot read or understand the deception they have just perpetrated. The following is my own personal account taken from my own "Individual Master File" that I obtained through the "Freedom of Information Act".

The following is a letter written by me, to the agent of the, Internal Revenue Service, in Idaho Falls, Idaho, explaining to him what I had found out about my IMF(Individual Master File): dated February 10, 1999

Mr. Mason,

"I am writing in response to the notice of intent to levy which appears to come from your office. I am responding as the notice requests. I disagree with this notice and request an appeal because of the following violations of law. I am not an attorney and will attempt to convey the facts clearly as possible so as not to confuse you."

"I do not think you are aware of what has occurred in my case and do not hold you responsible up to today. I have obtained a copy of my Individual Master File for the years 1993, 1994 and 1995 and have decoded the file which revealed the following. I have marked the IMF to help explain what has occurred. Looking at the IMF I have located the document locator number and marked it for identification as number "1". Please note the attached document from the IRS marked as "A" for identification. The 9th digit identifies the first number of the blocking series, now look at the document from the IRS marked with a "B" for identification and you will see that the first digit in the blocking series identifies the true tax class. The 9th digit in my DLN is a two which is also the first digit of the blocking series. Comparing this number with the document from the IRS marked "C" for identification and you will see that the series 200 through 299 are "**non-taxable 1040's**".

"The second issue marked on my IMF as "2" for identification and according to the IRS is the transaction code which identifies the type of tax. The number on my IMF is a "**150**" which has been identified by the IRS as a transaction code for self-employed income in the **Virgin Islands**. This is evidenced by the documents from the IRS marked "D" and "E" for identification. I don't know if you are aware but I have never worked in the Virgin Islands and have received absolutely no income from such a source. There are other entries which give undisputed evidence of **fraud** and you are now aware and must stop immediately".

"Also I understand that the Internal Revenue Code imposes a tax on all citizens of the United States, within the jurisdiction of the United States. [26 CFR 1.1-1] I do not believe this includes me because the Internal Revenue Code at section 7701(a)(9) and (10) do not include the 50 states. These subsections define the term United States and States and according to the opening section subparagraph of 7701(a) clearly instructs the reader that the definition is restrictive unless otherwise stated."

"I went to section 7701 because I find that Title 4 U.S.C.~71&72 state as follows: ~71 establishes the seat of the United States Government within borders of the District of Columbia; ~72 specifies that no department of government attached to the seat of government can operate beyond the borders of the District of Columbia except as specifically authorized by statute."

"I have found other sections with definitions of United States and the "50 states" were included for those purposes. For instance, section 46112(a)(4) relative to petroleum, in defining the term "United States" means the **50 States**, the District of Columbia, the Commonwealth of Puerto Rico, any possession of the United States, the Commonwealth of the Northern Mariana Islands, and the Trust Territory of the Pacific Islands. Here you can easily see the term United States includes the "50 States" along with the other definitions defined at section 7701(a)(9) and (10)."

"Another definition, at section 6103(b)(5)(A) relative to exchanging information the term "state" is defined as : "any of the **50 states**, the District of Columbia, the Commonwealth of Puerto Rico, the Virgin Islands, the Canal Zone, Guam, American Samoa, and the Commonwealth of the Northern Mariana Islands". Here again the term "50 states" is clearly defined along with the other definitions at 7701(a)(10)."

"The legal definition of the "United States" has changed every time a territory of the United States has become a sovereign state of the union. See Alaska Omnibus Act, P.L. 86-70, 73 Stat. 141; Hawaii Omnibus Act, P.L. 86-624, 74 Stat. 411; and the changes in the definitions for "United States" in the different editions of the Internal Revenue Code (IRC) before and after these territories were admitted into the union as sovereign states. We found in these acts that after these two states were added to the 50 states they were removed from the definition of United States in the Internal Revenue Code."

"I could also not have received any taxable wages because the regulations show the wages received from the fifty states **are not taxable**. 26 CFR 31,3121(e)-1 in defining the term United States and state as follows:

(a) When used in the regulations in this subpart, the term "State" includes the District of Columbia, the Commonwealth of Puerto Rico, the Virgin Islands, the Territories of Alaska and Hawaii before their admission as States, and(when used with respect to services performed after 1960), Guam and American Samoa,"

(b) When used in the regulations in this subpart, the term "United States", when used in a geographical sense, means the several states (including the Territories of Alaska and Hawaii before their admission as States), the District of Columbia, the Commonwealth of Puerto Rico, and the Virgin Islands. When used in the regulations in this subpart with respect to services performed after 1960, the term "United States" also includes Guam and American Samoa when the term is used in a geographical sense. The term "citizen of the United States" includes a citizen of the Commonwealth of Puerto Rico or the Virgin Islands, and, effective January 1, 1961, a citizen of Guam or American Samoa."

"This clearly demonstrates that the fifty states have been removed from the definition of United States and State."

"Because of these issues and the fact that I do not fit into the definition of "**taxpayer**" as defined at 7701(a)(14) and 1313(b) I have no tax liability for filing requirement. I have since found that someone filed substitute returns and created a **1040 tax liability** for me. Again, see my **IMF** at the location marked "2" and you will find a "SFR" followed by the **"150"** and the date.[06021997] This means that someone filed a substitute return for Virgin Island tax liability. These returns were apparently filed pursuant to IRC section 6020(b) by someone. I have not seen any such return which would allow me to appeal such a finding pursuant to IRC section 5293.2 I have also found that the person who filed these alleged returns did in fact **violate** the law."

"IRC section 5293.1 states that if a taxpayer fails to file employment, excise, or partnership returns then the returns may be filed for them pursuant to 6020(b). I have no employment, excise or partnership returns to file. I also found that the national delegation order from the Secretary regarding filing of returns allows the filing of **only** the following forms, 941, 720, 2290, CT-1, 1065, 11-B, 942 and 943. There is no delegation order allowing for the filing of a 1040 form pursuant to section 6020(b) for a person in the fifty states."

"As I stated earlier, I could not have received any taxable wages or income because 26 CFR 31.3121(b)-3 states that **to be** taxable, the wages must be received from employment **within** the United States. This CFR instructed me to turn to CFR 31.3121(e)-1 for the definition of United States. Paragraph (c) of this same part states that services performed outside the United States as defined under Part 31.3121(e)-1 do not constitute employment. Part 31.3121(e)-1 defines State, United States and citizen as stated above. I could not by law receive any taxable wages in any of the years because I lived **in one of the freely associated fifty united states.**"

"Then reading 26 CFR 1.861-1(c) which states: "Determination of taxable income. The taxable income from sources within or without the United States will be determined under the rules of

Sections 1.861-8 through 1.861-14 for determining taxable income from sources within the United States". 26 CFR 1.861-8(a)(4) states: "Statutory grouping of gross income...for the purposes of this section, the term "statutory grouping" means the gross income from a <u>specific source</u> or activity which <u>must first be determined to arrive at "taxable income"</u>; from which <u>specific</u> source or activity under an operative section. (See paragraph (f)(1) of this section. After reading 26 CFR 861-8(f)(1) I find that I am not nor **ever have been in a taxable activity** nor did I receive any taxable income."

"As noted above, someone has **falsified** the records held by the IRS, specifically my IMF file as noted above. To reiterate, I found that someone has classified me with a transaction code "150" and according to the impute manual 6209 transaction code "150" is for a **Virgin Island** activity. As you know, I live in Idaho and have no contacts with the Virgin Islands. This in itself is **fraud** or at least a violation of Title 18 U.S.C. Section 1001."

This list of violations go on and on including, as noted above the filing of a substitute 1040 when the IRS documents have been coded in our files that we have a "non-taxable 1040". And pursuant to delegation order number 182, authorizing the filing of substitute returns, there is no authority to file a substitute 1040."

"I want you to stop all collection action and notify me of this. I will be glad to send you the remaining documentation that shows additional fraud. Be informed that you may be personally liable for your failure to comply with this request. To attempt to continue any collection actions knowing there may be a violation of law or in violation of **my rights** would be a **criminal act**. Therefore, consider this letter as **constructive notice** that Title 18 of U.S.C. Says if any federal employee deprived any citizen of his right to privacy or any other constitutional rights, then that citizen can sue the federal employee in their personal capacity, if he notifies that employee in advance of his intentions to do so, and that if my constitutional rights are violated, I will avail myself of this remedy. The new taxpayers' bill of rights also makes an agent personally liable up to $100,000.00 for any action that were knowingly committed."

"I have sent a FOIA request to Scott Duncan requesting my AMDISA file which will show additional violation. I will send you these as soon as I get them. I may also file affidavits with the Justice Department and the Federal Grand Jury requesting an investigation. You must understand, if I cannot get this corrected immediately, I may file a Quo Warranto petition to force you to bring forth your authority and to bring the **fraud** committed against me before a judge. The Inspector General has advised me I can file a complaint with him also. I will wait 15 days to allow you time to contact me before I take other action. Respectfully, Steven Sego."

Note: I stopped filing in 1993, and this fraudulent account someone created for me as the IMF was done in June of 1997. One further precaution I indulged in, was to write to the District of

Columbia to inquire of our Federal Government, as to whether or not if there were any "tax liens" against me or my wife. Written to: "Government of the District of Columbia", office of the Chief Financial Officer, Office of Tax and Revenue". They replied with a certificate, notarized and signed. It states: "**CERTIFICATE**", This is to certify that as of this 10th day of June, 1998, there Does not appear of record in the Recorder of Deeds Division for the District of Columbia **Any** U.S. Tax Liens against *Steven* Sego"... signed and notarized.

The only way to break this account is to stop filing your fraudulent 1040 Form every year. Never file it again, since you have found out that you are 1) not a resident or citizen of the United States of America corporation; 2) you are a "natural born" or "naturalized" citizen under the Constitution of the several "united states of America"-Republic and under God; 3) You are not involved in the commercial aspect of buying or selling alcohol, tobacco or firearms; 4) You are not a "taxpayer; 5) The 1040 form is a fraudulent form, and you are not required to file it; 6) There is no law requiring you to file it; 7) The IRS has no police powers, and only has any authority in "admiralty jurisdiction", and only when the issue at hand involves the business transactions of buying or selling alcohol, tobacco or firearms; 8) The IRS are themselves, a private corporation, and is not an agency of the federal government, and neither is the Federal Reserve Bank, as it also is a private corporation.

The IRS was first incorporated in 1933 in the state of Delaware, and since have moved their headquarters off shore of the 50 states, to the Territory of Puerto Rico. The IRS is a private corporation, and as a corporation, is under the federal jurisdiction, or Admiralty Jurisdiction. This in itself shows that the IRS has no jurisdiction in the several United States. The IRS only has jurisdiction if you incorporate your business, or you file and invite them into your lives. The IRS is a break off of the Federal Reserve Bank and is the strong arm or collection agency for this bank. Evidence of this, is if you have ever paid taxes to the IRS by check. Later you received back the voided check, after it cleared, and on the back of it is stamped: "deposited with the Federal Reserve Bank".

The main purpose of the IRS, is to gather interest payments for the Federal Reserve Bank. These interest payments are made on their privately created fiat money that we carry in our wallets every day, in different forms. As long as we continue to use this form of monetary system, then we are in debt to the Federal Reserve Bank for the use of this fiat money.

With every debt, there is a required interest to be collected. Ask yourself, have I ever paid interest on what I consider my own money? The interest is collected in the form of Income Tax, from an ignorant people, by a cunning and socialist agency, the IRS, being the collection arm of the Federal Reserve Bank. What is really ironic, is that our United States government pays the Federal Reserve, money for every bill printed, then turns around and allows the Federal Reserve to collect interest payments on these I.O.U.'s also, from we the people, making slaves out of those who prefer to be ignorant. Do not be fooled into believing that the IRS is part of the Federal government, or that paying the IRS is supporting the government to operate. It is absolutely not true.

So, as it seems, we are pushed to the brink of easily having a communist/socialist government takeover in America. We are standing, as it were on the precipice of a deep chasm. In order to push us away from this great gulf, we need to dismantle the ten planks of the communist manifesto. We must steadily and diligently, every time we get good people into office as President, Congressmen and women etc... This should be our major goal, but most importantly, staying close to our Heavenly Father.

There is one important point to remember, and it is this: One man can make a difference in this fight for Freedom. Here is the last eight lines of a poem I wish to include that will drive this point home:

Title: "I AM JUST ONE MAN"

"...I know that one man cannot save the day,

So give me a break and get out of my way,

And go tell your stories to someone who's brave,

For I find it easy to just be a slave.

Across all the land ten million men cried,

And all of them fed on the very same lies.

And evil has triumphed for nothing was done,

While ten million men said, "I'm only one."

By Jay Merrill.

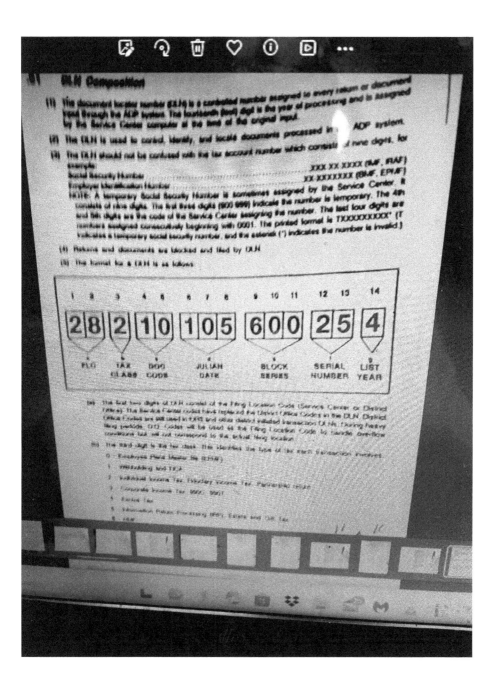

Ann Arbor News

IRS: Lack of enforcement is resulting in the loss of billions in revenue, tax experts say

USA TODAY Washington

02/02/00 Updated 11:50 PM ET

Reformed IRS: Seizures down 98%

By Owen Ullmann, USA TODAY

WASHINGTON -- Internal Revenue Service audits and enforcement actions to collect back taxes have plummeted since passage of a law in 1998 intended to curb IRS abuses, the agency said Wednesday.

From 1997 to 1999, property seizures fell 98%, garnishments on wages and bank accounts were down 86% and liens on assets declined 69%, officials testified at a hearing of the Senate Finance Committee.

7/13/01

United Nations and the military are enforced, programs and their directives are enforced, insure that their directives are enforced.

The highest risk for resistance to these United Nations directives will come from the American people who do not want to see their liberties taken from them. We have newspaper reports and our Northpoint Team sightings of these "UN" operations from all over the United States. Half of the troops at Fort Bragg, North Carolina, for instance, are today Russian soldiers. These are A.I.D. "UN" operations. Soviet T-72 tanks have been seen on railroad cars, and heavy trucks, in dozens of places across America within the last year. What is their purpose according to Senate Report No. 93-549, page 185? Are you sitting down, members of the jury?

The purpose of this IRS Principal, for whom the IRS collects the American tribute, is to promote, implement, and enforce absolute United Nations control over finance in The United States." •

No one is liable on an instrument unless and until he has signed it.

The long-winded comment following that straightforward statement makes it very clear, in the context of our study of the Internal Revenue Service, Inc. and its presentments and demands on behalf of its Principal, the Agency For International Development of the United Nations, that no one can be compelled to specific performance by any implied contract. In the Uniform Commercial Code there are no implied contracts permitted, and if properly and timely challenged by a defendant, every court or tribunal is obliged to rule in the defendant's favor or it is reversible error.

Section 3-401:1 goes on to state that "a signature" can be anything that is used for that purpose, such as a mark or

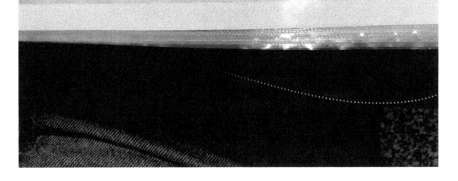

•"It appears from the documentary evidence, and inside information made available to me, that the Internal Revenue Service, Inc. agents are in fact "Agents of a Foreign Principal" within the meaning and intent of the "Foreign Agents Registration Act of 1938." They are directed and controlled by the corporate "Governor" of "The Fund." This means the International Monetary Fund. The Governor is also known as the "Secretary of Treasury." This information is available in a number of places:
Public Law 94-564 p. 5942 (1973); U.S. Government Manual, 1990/91 p. 480-481;
26 U.S.C.A 7701 (a) (11); Treasury Delegation Order No. 150-10;
22 U. S. C. A 611 (c) (iii); Legislative History, p. 5942; and Ron Paul Money Book (1991).
It gets worse! Because of its United Nations responsibilities, the Internal Revenue Service, Inc. is also an agency of the International Criminal Police Organization, [INTERPOL] and the IRS solicits and collects information from, and on behalf of, 150 Foreign Powers. It will assist any foreign police agency with data from your 1040 Label Forms. How else can it aid international development?
22 U.S.C.A 263a; The U.S. Government Manual 1990/91 p. 385; 22 U.S.C.A 285g and 287j;
26 U.S.C.A 6103 (k) (4).
Treasury Delegation Order No. 92 states that the Internal Revenue Service, Inc. people are trained under the Division of Human Resources and the IRS Commissioner, by the Office of Personnel Management. Look in the 1976 Edition of 22 U.S.C.A. 287, 1979 Supp. III p. 474 and you will find Executive Order No. 10422. It states that the Office of Personnel Management, the very agency which trains new IRS operatives, apparently such as the unregistered IRS Foreign Agent who recently stated that he "will get Nord Davis, no matter what it takes," is under the direction of the Secretary General of the United Nations. Some Americans may think that this is just wonderful. I do not! My special appreciation to patriot John Nelson of Colorado for some of the research information provided here.

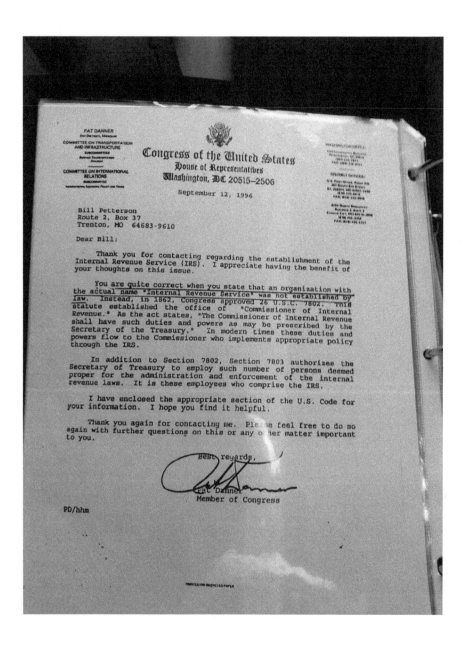

CHAPTER 7
Sovereignty-The Sovereign Citizen

The word *"Sovereignty, or Sovereign"*, is used when describing a king or powerful government body. God is described as being *Sovereign,* and all powerful and mighty. It is a term of respect and dignity. Christ is described as *"Sovereign Lord"*. He is the King of kings, the Lord of Lords, Wonderful, Councilor, the Mighty God. *"17. For the Lord your God is **God of gods**, and **Lord of lords**, a great God, a mighty, and a terrible, which regardeth not persons, nor taketh reward;" (Deuteronomy 10:17, KJV)* In other words, God is no respecter of persons, in regard to rank, wealth, color, nationality, or otherwise, and he cannot be bribed or bought for favors, and he is all powerful.

*"5. And from Jesus Christ, who is the faithful witness, and the first begotten of the dead, and the **prince of the kings** of the earth. Unto him that loved us, and washed us from our sins in his own blood," (**1 Timothy** 6:15, KJV)*

*"15. Which in his times he shall shew who is blessed and **only Potentate**, the **King of kings**, and **Lord of lords**;" (Revelation 1:5, KJV)*

When King Nebuchadnezzar, was talking to Daniel, after Daniel interpreted his dream for him, he said: *"47. The King answered unto Daniel, and said, Of a truth it is, that your God is* **God of Gods,** *and a* **Lord of Kings**, *and a revealer of secrets, seeing thou couldest reveal this secret."(Daniel 2:47, KJV)*

We are not to fear as we endure this life, for God is all seeing and he has already won the war and he promises, that it is he, who will stand up and defend those who are doing his will, against those who are in open rebellion against him. He never promised that his people would not have trials and hardship, but the beauty of God's love is, that when we fall, he will be right there to pick us up again, and dust us off. He normally does this through his people helping one another.

The evil IRS is just one of those agencies, combined with the people who work for them, that are making war with God. They violate the work of God, and the free agency that God has given to we the people, as "unalienable rights". *"14. These shall make war with the Lamb, and the Lamb shall overcome them: for he is the* **Lord of lords**, *and* **King of kings**: *and they that are with him are called, and chosen, and faithful." (Revelation 17:14, KJV)* The ones who are called and chosen and faithful, are the ones who received the gospel of Jesus Christ, and obey his commandments, and have become the "sons and daughters of God".

"12. His eyes were as flames of fire, and on his head were many **crowns**; *and he had a name written, that no man knew, but he himself." "13. And he was clothed with a vesture dipped in blood:*

and his name is called the **WORD OF GOD***.*" "*14. And the armies which were in heaven followed him upon white horses, clothed in fine linen, white and clean.*" "*15 And out of his mouth goeth a sharp sword, that with it he shall smite the nations: and he shall* **rule them** *with a rod of iron: and he* **treadeth the winepress** *of the fierceness and wrath of* **Almighty God.**" "*16. And he hath on his vesture and on his thigh a name written,* **KING OF KINGS, AND LORD OF LORDS***.*" *(Revelation 19:12-16, KJV)*

The scriptures ask the question: "*5. Who is like unto the Lord our God, who dwelleth on high,*" *(Psalms 113:5, KJV)*

"*18. To whom then will ye* **liken God?** *Or what likeness will ye* **compare unto him?**" *(Isaiah 40:18, KJV)*

Knowing these things about God and Jesus Christ, then you get the understanding that God is the best example of Sovereignty that you can imagine. So just thinking about it, you begin to realize that, if we truly are the children of God, and his literal offspring, then we are also like him, and are "Sovereign" under his law, and his law is the Constitution, for the Constitution embodies the commandments of God. That means that if we do what Christ tells us to do, receive him and by receiving him, we receive his gospel of truth, and live it, then we too, may be sovereign citizens, even while we are here on earth. God has not left us alone, but it takes courage and endurance to the end, in order to weather the storm of the devil. We may become sons and daughters of God, and by being such, are

Sovereign by virtue of this relationship.

What does it mean to be "Sovereign"? *"6. and has made **us** kings and priests to His God and Father, and to Him be glory and dominion forever and ever. Amen." (Revelation 1:6, KJV)*

Black's Law Dictionary, 6th Edition gives the definition of "**Sovereign**": "A **person**, body, or state in which independent and supreme authority is vested; a chief ruler with supreme power; **a king** or other ruler in a monarchy." "'**Sovereign people**': The political body, consisting of the entire number of citizens and qualified electors, who, in their collective capacity, possess the powers of sovereignty and exercise them through their chosen representatives."

The Constitution of the united states of America-Republic, under God, is what makes us free and independent, guaranteeing us with **"unalienable rights"**, endowed upon the sons and daughters of God, by God, through the virtue of first, being related to Him, as he is the "Supreme Ruler" of heaven and earth. Second, He has given us freedom, if we are wise enough to hold onto it, through obedience to *His,* commandments. We are given the right to be sovereign. We the people, independently and collectively under the Constitution, have the power to govern ourselves freely, with absolute power in our homes and lives, as long as we do not harm other persons or property.

We have the right to Life, Liberty, and the Pursuit of Happiness. We have the right and freedom to cast our own votes to elect representatives to represent us collectively. We have the right to voice our opinions, the freedom of speech, the right to religion, to bear arms, to even declare and wage war. We have the right to a redress of grievances, etc... These are blessings only **kings** could have. Under the Constitution, we are made **"kings and queens"** in the united states of America-Republic.

When Christ was fasting forty days and forty nights, Lucifer came to him while he was in his weakest moments and tried to tempt Christ into giving Satan jurisdiction over him. Christ, however, refrained and beat the Devil at his own game. Jurisdiction is everything.

Adam, by giving Satan jurisdiction over him while he was in the Garden of Eden, is why he fell, but that was the plan, so that we, His children, might be able to have this life and choose between right and wrong. The plan also included, that Christ would overcome the devil, or the world/Hell, thus, enabling us to someday return back into the presence of our Heavenly Father, and He has shown us the way to do it.

When the IRS comes after an individual for income taxes, they do so at first in "Admiralty Jurisdiction". They come at you with the appearance of force, by trying to scare you, as Satan did to Christ. They use threat, duress, deceit and coercion. Their hopes are to scare you into what they call voluntarily of yourself, giving personal information and evidence against yourself, that is incriminating, thus, causing you to waive your Constitutional Rights.

Once you take your kingly, or queenly crown off of your head, and surrender your sovereignty over to them, they then have gotten jurisdiction over you, and then proceed against you through the courts in civil proceedings. To be "Sovereign", does not require special papers to be filed by you, though a paper trail helps you establish your thinking and intent, and could be helpful. The only requirements you need though, in order to be a "sovereign citizen", is to know who you are. If you are a natural born citizen of the American-Republic, then by birth you are Sovereign. If you are naturalized into the American Republic, domiciled into one of the several states, then you can claim sovereignty.

If you are naturalized into the United States of America, or a citizen of the United States of America, or a resident of the United States of America, a citizen of Puerto Rico, Guam, Virgin Islands, American Samoa or other territory, then you are not a sovereign citizen in America. You are the corporate person, and are under Admiralty Jurisdiction.

This "corporate person" is often referred to as our, *"Straw Man"*, name all in capital letters. The IRS just assumes you are this corporate person unless you assert your Constitutional Rights, to the contrary. When you can exhibit a certain degree of knowledge, then they can have no control over you. When you can see the whole picture, then you have the power over them,

There is no requirement for you to file specific paperwork, for you to be a Sovereign Citizen. The only requirement necessary, is that you personally have to walk by faith in Jesus Christ, know who you are, and gain knowledge and understanding. That way, you can be like Christ and resist, and refuse the jurisdiction of the devil, and the devil's minions, and temptations.

We must know in which kingdom we belong and are part of. Knowledge is the key, as the Bible talks about: *"6. My people are destroyed from lack of knowledge"* (*Hosea 4:6, KJV*) There is no paperwork in the world that will make you sovereign. Your birth certificate or naturalization papers point the way, here in America-Republic, as to your desired sovereignty, but even then is only worldly documentation, and can't be taken with you when you die. To be "Sovereign" is a frame of mind.

If you are a "natural born citizen", or a "naturalized citizen", you are now protected under the Constitution of the United States of America, in mortality. The Constitution was written "Of the People", "For the People", and "By the People", to the Federal Government, telling it that this is the way it is. We told the government that this is the limits of government, and it is to stay within the boundaries set by the Constitution. Under the Constitution, "We the People" are free, like Kings and Queens, and it makes government the "Servant".

It is not necessary for we the people, to be afraid of the servant. The servant is to answer to "we the people".

Now a "naturalized citizen", you need to learn how to assert your rights, the same as a "natural born citizen". Honestly, there are so many people born in America, who take for granted what they have. They miss the blessings God has bestowed upon them, usually because of selfishness, personal gratification, or ignorance. They miss what it means to really live, to really be Free. Freedom is what is so precious, and is to be treasured above anything else, worlds without end.

CHAPTER 8
Romans Chapter 13

The Liberals will use Romans: Chapter 13, to justify their unjust laws and evil practices, when it suits their purposes. They only refer to the <u>Bible</u> if, and when it fits into their agenda, and serves their purposes, while trying to convince the Christian to buy into their obvious lies.

We need to understand, that when Paul wrote the <u>Book of Romans,</u> that he was concerned about the people rising up against their government, thus causing chaos and anarchy. His main concern was preaching the gospel of Jesus Christ to the people, thus converting many, and possibly, even the heads of governments, kings, even emperors, into believing in Christ.

In Paul's day, all of the countries were liberal, and had in place systems of force. To go against the laws openly would have been a sure-fire way of bringing the powers that be, down on them in a bloody confrontation. The best solution, was first educate the people, including, and especially those in high places. If any fighting was to be done It would be from the wicked warring against the wicked.

There are many of those times when the laws of man are in complete contradiction with the laws of God. So in this case, do you follow man's law or the commandments of God? Daniel, in the <u>Bible,</u>

showed a great example of what to do in a case of this kind. He didn't stop praying to his God because a king made a law that no one should pray to any God, other than the king for thirty days. Daniel had no choice but to ignore that edict, as it was in complete contradiction to what he knew was right, and if he put man first, then he would have dishonored his God. Ultimately, Daniel was thrown into the lion's den, but did not God defend Daniel because he was right? Through Daniel's example, God was glorified, Daniel was exonerated, and many people, including the King, Darius, turned to the God of Daniel.

Another great example of this, is in Meshack, Shadrack, and Abednego, the three friends of Daniel. They were all thrown into a fiery furnace for defying the law of Nebechadnezzar, who tried to take away the people's right to worship to their God, who is in Heaven. They refused, and consequently were thrown into the furnace, and while in there, were visited by a fourth man, Christ, and came out with not so much as the smell of smoke upon them.

To obey all rulers and laws without question is unthinkable, as most rulers, because they get a little power as they suppose, begin to exercise unrighteous dominion upon their subjects. Are we to support "Roe v. Wade", because it is a Supreme Court decision that is construed by evil people to kill all of the unborn babies, children of God, that it has through the years? Their sense of fairness goes out the window, and selfishness comes in. When evil laws are in place, the people's first responsibility is to exercise all other options peaceably to change these laws. When all other options fail, then the people have the right by God to rise up and put off such repressive government.

Verse-6 of Romans: 13, talks about paying **tribute**: *"6. For for this cause pay ye tribute also: for they are God's ministers, attending continually upon this very thing." "7. Render therefore to all their dues; custom to whom custom; fear to whom fear; honour to whom honour."(Roman 13:6, KJV)*

Every government needs to collect taxes to run their country. It can't be run smoothly without funds to operate, and so there is a necessity of tribute and to contribute. As this scripture states: render just dues according as is proper. Customs to whom is appropriate, tribute to whom respect is due, and excise to whom honour is due. However, the laws will advocate the tax to be allocated in any government's law, whether just, or unjust, making it the law. In America's case, this law is the Constitution.

Today, America stands as the only remaining bastion of Freedom. America is the only country in the world that is "free by law". The "supreme law of the land" is the Constitution. It is a law "Of the People", "By the People", and "For the People". It's laws are having the "Ten Commandments" embodied into it. The Constitution is just dripping with **God** all through it. The rules and laws in America are made by We the People, and we insist on the

"Rule of Law".

In the Constitution, there are only three lawful forms of taxes. The first two being import taxes and export taxes. "Tribute" is collected by the foreign country receiving the exports, and "customs" are paid by the country receiving the imports. The third form of tax to the support of our government, that all of the people pay. This third form of tax that all of the people contribute and participate in is, Excise taxes. This tax is the users' tax, meaning, if we use something, then at that time we pay for it. These three taxes, in and of themselves, are designed to more than support both state and federal governments. The fuel tax alone carries 47 different federal excise taxes. This is just one of the many excise taxes that not only fund government, but also limits the size of government.

Imports and exports are paid by corporations of governments, both receiving and exporting goods from their own countries, and by paying taxes to the receiving country. The excise tax is the payment of taxes on the goods of the receiving country by the populace of that country, who are the consumers of the product shipped. Excise tax is a tax put on the product, for the consumer to participate in helping the shipping corporation to offset costs of their product, and for the transportation of it. In other words, if you want to use the product, then you must pay for it. You are paying for what the product is worth to the corporation or persons responsible for producing it, plus a sales tax added to go toward helping your government offset their costs as well. These taxes are lawful and reasonable. Anything more than these three lawful taxes make slaves of the people, and rob them of their labor and their wealth. The Constitution is Caesar today, in America.

The income tax is nowhere in the first 13 articles in the Bill of Rights, that We the People wrote. The 14th Amendment through the 16th Amendment and beyond, are all written by the federal government, for the federal government, all done by manipulation of self-serving Liberals, with the agenda of destroying our country, and diminishing "We the People's" basic personal liberties. As proven here in the chapters of this book, the 16th Amendment only applies to the corporate persons, in this case ignorant liberals/democrats, willing to be slaves of a despotic government, and those wanting a king over themselves, and all people. They are not satisfied with just themselves being miserable, but insist on everyone being miserable with them.

If the rulers of countries, are good rulers, and want to do right by the people, then the people are obligated to obey the laws, because they are probably good laws. If, however, the rulers are evil, as we know the Democrats and pretending GOP Republicans are, then we the people have the duty to resist.

"1. Let every soul be subject unto the higher powers. For there is no power but of God: the powers that be are ordained of God." This is true, as "Almighty God", is the supreme power, and he sets

up kings and he takes down kings at his pleasure. He commands kings to rule with justice and mercy over the people, and when they don't, God brings them down.

When a king or any ruler is evil, and their decrees and laws are evil, then the people must resist as Daniel, Meshack, Shadrack, and Abednego did. Therefore verse 2 of Romans cannot be true, or does not apply to certain situations, because God blessed them, and did not damn them. So, to read Romans Chapter 13, and assume that Paul is talking about all kings, kingdoms and countries the same, is a wrong analysis, even though the principle is the same. We must learn to liken the scriptures unto ourselves, in our circumstances, and in our time.

To have law and order is a must, but when the people's most basic rights are trampled underfoot, "right to religion/worship, right to choose, right of conscience, right to work, right to life, etc., then the people in any government must look the devil in the eye, and say NO!

"We the People", in America, are the "kings and queens". We wrote the Constitution as the "Supreme Law of the Land", and when evil rulers in our country try to usurp power, write bad laws to enslave we the people, then we must resist.

"But when a long train of abuses and usurpations, pursuing invariable the same Object, evinces a design to reduce them under

*absolute Despotism, it **is their right, it is their duty, to throw off such Government, and to provide new Guards for their future security...**" (see* Declaration of Independence).

In fact, it is a strict commandment from God, that we defend our "Freedom", and our families, even unto bloodshed if necessary. *"9. And now the design of the Nephites was to support their lands, and their houses, and their wives, and their children, that they might preserve them from the hands of their enemies; and also that they might preserve their **rights** and their privileges, yea, and also their **liberty**, that they might **worship God** according to their desires."* *"47. And again, the Lord has said that: Ye shall defend your **families even unto bloodshed**. Therefore for this cause were the Nephites contending with the Lamanites, to defend **themselves**, and their **families**, and their **lands**, their **country**, and their rights, and their **religion**." (Alma 43:9,47. Book of Mormon)*

Any minister, pastor, prophet, leader, teacher, doctor of divinity etc., that tries to tell the people that bad laws are to be followed that enslave the people, then those leaders are not of God. The IRS, and what they represent, is just one of those huge lies that the leaders of the churches want you to believe is okay.

The Mormons embrace the IRS agents with open arms, along with lying Democrats, and give them temple recommends to go to their temples, as if they will be saved in the kingdom of God. There are even many Democrats in top leadership positions in the church.

For the people to be ignorant and blind, is the way slaves are made. We must recognize and resist the lies, and cling to the truth, as truth is the "light of Christ". In no way can we expect to go to God unless we have this light. We must be involved in good causes, namely, to defeat the slaughter of our unborn children, brought about by Roe v. Wade. This Supreme Court case, pushed through by the evil Democrats, has made it legal to kill our children. Every year thousands of abortions are performed by liberal doctors, because of this ruling. If we as Christians don't resist this abomination, then we are killers ourselves, and the blood of the innocent is on our hands as well.

What Paul is talking about in Romans Chapter 13, must be taken in the spirit it was intended, and all men must liken the scriptures unto themselves and exercise the freedom of reason, and good conscience. You can't often find people in government who, one hundred percent, have the people's best interest at heart. You will never find a Democrat in government who cares a bit about your liberty, but only their own selfish agenda.

Paul is assuming in Romans 13:3, that all rulers are good, and are a terror to the evil. We all know from sad experience, that very few rulers of countries worldwide are good. Today in 2020, in America, to have a Democrat get into any office in the land is true grief and a terror to the good. We remember what the Democrats and liberals stand for, and how they destroy everything they touch.

Is Paul telling us that we are to give up our freedoms despite who gets into office in the land, who tramples on the Constitution, who won't uphold their "oath of office"? He is not saying that at all, however, the liberals would love for the clergy to interpret it that way. That is why the Democrats under Obama organized the "Clergy Response Team".

Thousands if not millions of pastors, popes, bishops, prophets, ministers, teachers etc., have joined together under their 501(c)(3) charters, in agreement to support the liberals in calming their congregations, by preaching about Romans chapter 13, in case of a national emergency, or martial law. The purpose is to make their people believe that what their governments are doing, whether good or bad, is from God.

It was a travesty when Hitler was in power, and was the cause of killing so many Jewish people. Also Stallin, and Lennon, are responsible for the murder of millions of people who they deemed as opposition. Even the Catholic Church down through the dark ages, and the innumerable people killed and burned at the stake, for defying their empire. Is Paul telling the people that they are not to resist evil? If he is, then he is directly contradicting God, and I know he is not doing that. We must stay close to God ourselves, by having this "Light of Christ". We must be armed with knowledge in these last days, so as not to be deceived.

*"7. Submit yourselves therefore to God. **Resist the devil** and he*

will flee from you."(James 4:7, KJV) We must be about God's business, so that we are not found mingling with the goats, and found wanting when Christ comes again.

Another good example of good people resisting the wicked, is when Elijah defied King Ahab and Jezebel, when he cleansed Israel of the Priests of Baal. When Jezebel heard what had happened she wanted to catch and destroy Elijah, and Elijah fled to a cave near a creek, and a raven fed him every day. Elijah then learned that there were seven thousand more besides himself who defied Ahab and Jezebel.

Another is King David, when he avoided King Saul. Another is Moses, who in defense of an Israelite, killed an Egyptian, then fled. These are just a few among many, where, when men and women have seen injustice, and have acted against those who are in power. So those who would preach that all rulers are to be obeyed regardless of the circumstances, is a huge deception. Christ himself drove the wicked out of the temple with a whip, and overturned their tables. Christ is our prime example, let's do the things that we have seen him do.

John has this to say: *"1. Beloved, **believe not every spirit**, but try the spirits whether they are of God: because many **false prophets** are gone out into the world." (1 John 4:1, KJV)*

*"8. Beware lest any man spoil you through **philosophy** and vain*

*deceit, after the tradition of men, after the rudiments of the **world**, and not after Christ." (Colossians 2:8, KJV)*

"13. But evil men and seducers shall wax worse and worse, deceiving, and being deceived." (2 Timothy 3:13, KJV)

*"17. Now I beseech you, brethren, mark them which cause **division** and offenses **contrary to the doctrine** which we have learned; and avoid them." "18. For they that are such serve not our Lord Jesus Christ, but their own belly; and by good words and fair speeches deceive the hearts of the simple." (Romans 16:17-18, KJV)*

*"24. For there shall arise **false Christs, and false prophets**, and shall show great signs and wonders; insomuch that, if it were possible, they shall **deceive the very elect.**" (Matthew 24:24, KJV)*

Here is a few paragraphs by a, Sam Adams, from Brooksville, Florida, in his article, "Rendering Caesar His Due", "A Christian Response to the Income Tax":

"Most Christians in America believe it is their moral, legal, and Biblical duty to send in their form 1040's every April and pay what is known as the income tax, mistakenly believing they are *rendering to Caesar that which is his."* Many do so believing God will not hold them accountable for where the money is going or what type of destructive socialistic programs or other ungodly abortionists anti-Christian, anti-family or anti-American globalists agendas are being funded by their money. Many Christians are not at all bothered by the fact that all told their government asks for over five times the proportion of their earnings than Almighty God requires. And most Christians in America are sadly so ignorant of the Constitution and are so trusting in their increasingly secular humanist government that even when presented with the evidence, they refuse to believe that they in fact in most cases have no Biblical, moral, or legal duty to file a form 1040 or pay the "income tax.""

"In recent years, it has increasingly come to light that the American people have throughout most of this century been duped by what is probably the most colossal fraud ever perpetrated by any government against its own people. This fraud has resulted in a tyranny far worse than our founding fathers took up arms against or would have imagined could arise under the Constitution, they left to us. But tragically and to our extreme detriment, the Constitution, the supreme law of the land, is being ignored and by-passed by socialist and totalitarian forces in our government that are attempting to replace the Constitution with their own *"laws"* which are stripping us of the freedoms and *"unalienable rights"* our Christian forefathers were willing to fight and die for, and are quickly leading us to the brink of the absorption of America into the totalitarian "New World Order" global government of the antichrist."

"...Back to Matthew 22:21, *"Render therefore unto Caesar the things which are Caesar's; and unto God, the things that are God's"*. Now, as the Apostle Peter said, *"gird up your mind for action"*:

<u>Filing a 1040 and paying the income tax is NOT rendering to Caesar!</u>
Every Christian desiring to be obedient to the Lord's directive in
Matthew 22:21 must answer this question, **Who is Caesar in
America?** At the time of Christ, Caesar himself represented the
highest civil law of the Roman Empire. The Roman Senate had long
since lost its political power, the republic had become a dictatorship
and Caesar ruled by decree. But who is Caesar in America? Is it the
President? Is it the Congress? The Supreme Court? Let us help you
with the answer: **the highest law of the land in America is the
CONSTITUTION**. Every branch of the Federal government
answers to the Constitution. In 1803, the Supreme Court ruled that
"all laws which are repugnant to the Constitution are null and void."
(Marbury v. Madison, 5 US (2Cranch) 137, 174, 1700. in Norton v.
Shelby County, (118 US 425 p. 4416) the Supreme Court ruled that
*"an unconstitutional act is not law; it confers no rights; it imposes
no duties; affords no protection; it creates no office; it is in legal
contemplation; as inoperative as though it had never been passed."*
According to American Jurisprudence, volume 16, section 256, *The
general rule is that an unconstitutional statute though having the
form and name of law, is in reality no law but is wholly void, and
ineffective for any purpose since unconstitutionally dates from the
time of its enactment and not merely from the date of the decision so
branding it...No one is bound to obey an unconstitutional law and
no courts are bound to enforce it."* As has been clearly shown, the
manner in which the income tax laws are being misapplied to strip

our constitutional rights is in itself most unconstitutional. Most of the programs the income tax goes to pay for are most unconstitutional (welfare, social security system, foreign aid, U.N., Federal control of Education and Labor, etc.). The purpose for the income tax and for estate taxes in general is to plunder the wealth of America and use that wealth to fund the New World Order government or the Antichrist and to destroy the Constitution. Therefore, for an American citizen to continue to pay the income tax is not rendering to Caesar, but directly to Satan. Selah: Think on these things. "

"We must also force the IRS to obey its own laws and stop their reign of gestapo-like terror ruling by force of fear rather than by rule of law. Apparently, this can only be accomplished through resistance; *"resist the devil and he will flee from you."* There is a rising groundswell of patriotic Americans banding together to study the law and regain *"government of the people"* and to force the lawless bureaucrats back within the confines of the Constitution. Within this patriotic movement, several paralegal organizations have arisen to assist individuals desiring to be free from IRS tyranny and the social security system; and in spite of the few losses which have been publicized by the controlled media, there have been many victories. Recently, a Tennessee man named Lloyd Long was taken to court by the IRS and charged with willful failure to file a tax return for tax years 1989 and 90. Using the above legal arguments combined with other court decisions and the IR Code itself, Mr. Long's attorneys proved to the Chattanooga jury that Mr. Long as a US citizen is not liable to pay income tax and is in no way *"required by law"* to file tax returns, even though he had earnings over $49,000.00 for each year in question. Due to this and many other patriot successes the government is reportedly trying to save face and excuse itself from a very embarrassing and potentially costly situation by abolishing the current income tax and possibly replacing it with either a national sales tax or reduced flat rate (10-17%) income tax **(still unacceptable Constitutionally)** with the excuse that the tax laws are too complicated and "unenforceable". By the IRS's own admission 1 in 5 "taxpayers" have stopped filing 1040 forms."...

"...But as the great patriot known as the father of the American Revolution, Samuel Adams said, *"If men, through fear, fraud, or mistake, should in terms renounce or give up any natural right, the eternal law of reason and the grand end of society would absolutely vacate such renunciation. The **right to freedom being the gift of God**, It is not in the power of man to alienate this gift and **voluntarily become a slave.**"*

"Christians are not called to sit idly by and, wait for the rapture while society goes to hell. Christians have been called to action; first to evangelism, but also to oppose, to*" "root out and to pull down"* the rampant evil in our society (Jer. 1:10). Daniel 11:32-35 describes how the people of God are to oppose the kingdom of the Antichrist:

"And by smooth words he will corrupt those who act wickedly against the covenant, but the people that do know their God shall be strong, and do exploits." "With light comes, responsibility; every Christian must prayerfully consider his calling into this battle, counting the cost. The time has come for God's people to take action;" *"to stand fast therefore in the liberty wherewith Christ hath made us free, and be not entangled again with the yoke of bondage"* *(Galatians 5:1, KJV)* The call of Revelation 18:4 to get out of Babylon is now going out to the Church, *"come out of her, My people, that you be not partakes of her sins, and that ye receive not of her plagues."* God's people need to open their ears to hear."

CHAPTER 9
Personal Experiences with the IRS

In writing this book, it may appear to the reader that the author might not have had much adversity in dealing with the IRS, however, this chapter is to assure the reader that a lot of blood, sweat, and tears, have went into the gaining of the knowledge contained herein. I have seven notebooks full of my correspondence with the mighty IRS. I kept it as a paper trail, establishing my continued Refusal of their foreign-fiction-jurisdiction.

Since then, anytime I received something from them, I wouldn't even open their literature/letter, or acknowledge their authority or existence. What I did was simply write above my name and corresponding address: "Refused", "No such corporate person at this address" "Return to sender", and send it back to them. Sometimes, the postal delivery driver wouldn't return it for me without me putting it in another envelope and placing a new stamp on it, because of those things written on the envelope, was construed by them as writing another letter, and they wanted to make money on the business. Most of the time, however, they would just return to sender, no questions asked. If, however, they won't return it without the new envelope, and new stamp, then accommodate them. Pretty simple, but keep records.

Once you begin to understand the IRS, you realize just how powerless they really are. You then begin to treat them with the contempt that they deserve, as the liars and robbers that they really are.

It used to terrify me, when I first started my journey. Every time I received a letter from them, my heart would start pounding. One time in church, my wife just broke down in a puddle of tears, because of them. The uncertainty that they used to bring, the foreboding, the dark shadow that always preceded them and followed after them, was very unique. The threat, duress, and coercion that they represented was a burden, and a nuisance. However, the closer I stayed to God, and the faith that I exercised in His Son, Jesus Christ, made it bearable and worth continuing the fight. Remember, you can only go halfway into the forest before you start coming out again.

Throughout the years, while dealing with the IRS, they had come to my home two times to attempt taking my property from me. Both times they left with an empty sack. The first time, it was an IRS agent, by himself. As soon as he told me who he was, and that he was there to tell me that the IRS was going to take my property from me if I didn't cooperate, I didn't argue with him. I simply, and immediately told him to leave. He said, "Okay" and turned and left. If he had any authority to be there, he would have said so. By me telling him to leave immediately, gave him no jurisdiction, and by law he had to leave, as he was trespassing on private property, and if he refused to leave, I could have called the sheriff and had him arrested for trespassing. So he turned and left right away, almost running.

The second time, was after tax court, when the same agent, accompanied by another, came together, in the middle of the day to my home. They came when they thought that I would be at work. I believe that they were hoping to confront my wife by herself, and intimidate her. I just happened to be there though. I saw them coming, and when I stepped out onto the porch, they were caught off guard. The IRS agent started to tell me who he was. I told him, "I know who you are", and calling him by name. He said, "We are here to take your property if you won't cooperate with us." I didn't argue, I didn't say anything, except, "Leave", with emphasis. The agent was very surprised, and his voice faltered, as he said, "Okay".

The both of them turned on their heels and almost ran out of there. As they were leaving, I called after them, and said loudly, "and don't come back, because the only thing you are going to get, is a law-suit slapped against you so fast, it won't quit." You see, they had no warrant, no court order, no police power, and they had no jurisdiction, because I never at any time gave them any. Is all the IRS has is bluff. It was a blessing to have my wife there and witnessing the whole thing. It surprised her and gave her so much more confidence, just seeing the powerlessness the IRS really has.

After thinking about it for a while, realizing that this was the second time the IRS agent trespassed onto my property, after me telling him the first time to leave, I decided to go ahead and file a complaint against him in the Federal Court, which in Idaho is the 1st Judicial District, District Court. I filed it myself without an attorney, but if I had it to do over, I would use an attorney, because they know their way around in a courtroom much, much better. I got the complaint written and finished, along with the Summons, had it stamped and recorded into the District Court. I then sent the IRS agent's copy down to the Bonneville County Sheriff's department, along with the instructions and proper fee, for them to perfect service on the agent, being as he was in Idaho Falls, Idaho.

After about a week or so, I received a letter from the Sheriff of Bonneville County telling me that to serve the IRS agent in question was impossible, because he was nowhere to be found in the county. Meanwhile, the court itself, had sent notice to the IRS agent's office notifying him of the complaint against him. The court then forwarded me a copy of the fax from the agent's office telling them that the agent was not in the county, therefore could not accept service. After studying the fax, It showed that it was sent by the IRS agent himself, dated, and time stamped from his own fax machine, from his own office. His intention was to fool everyone into believing he couldn't be served, thus, to evade a law-suit.

I promptly wrote to the court explaining the situation and what

I had observed. The court ultimately made him answer the complaint and summons. If I had employed an attorney, who knew the process better, I probably could have held his feet to the fire a lot longer, and caused him the stress that he was so willing to cause others.

Consequently the case was dismissed for one defect or another. It just goes to show you though, how terrified of law-suits the IRS are, and to what lengths their agents will go, to hide from accountability. You would think that if they were above board, then they would have nothing to worry about.

You will find, that any correspondence you have with the IRS, will never have a name of an agent, as the person responsible, for making a demand on you. They are hiding, because they know that people in the know, want names to hold accountable, so they are very careful.

Just remember, if you don't file federal taxes, then you don't need to file State taxes either. When the IRS failed to collect on me, then the Idaho State Tax Commission kicked in to try their brand of intimidation tactics. The tax commissions from any State are simply other arms of the IRS, just a different name.

The Idaho State Tax Commission began by filing "Notice of Lien" against every property I owned or bought, and when it expired after five years then they would renew it with the Secretary of State. This was a tactic to harass me when I went to sell the property, because the "notice of lien" would show up on the "Title Report", and potential buyers would either shy away, or put pressure on me to pay the unlawful lien.

At this point I had a few options, 1) Sue the Tax Commission, which is very costly to myself: 2) Admit I owed the State, even though I owed them nothing, but once I did that, the IRS would be back into my life, which would be very costly, and might even bring charges of tax evasion; 3) Find other people who thought like I did, and who would pay cash in exchange for a "Quit Claim Deed" or a "Warranty Deed" from me, which would close the transaction; or 4) Wait the Idaho Tax Commission out, as their bogus liens only lasted five years, after which they would either have to renew it or, drop it altogether. You can just about bet, that these childish tax collectors are one-hundred-percent liberal Democrat. They don't know how to tell the truth.

You see, there are no State statutes in any State, for the issuance and enforcement of their "notices of lien", just as there are no statutes in the states codes for the enforcement of an IRS lien or levy, either one. So, when you get a "notice of lien", or a "notice of levy", just remember that it has no force in the law. One thing for dead certain is, that it is definitely not Constitutional. Unless you admit to owing either the IRS or the State Tax Commission anything, or you argue the amount they say you owe, you haven't given them jurisdiction. To argue over an amount they say you owe, is telling them that you might not owe what they say you owe, but to them you are saying you owe something.

There is a big difference between the "land tax", and an IRS lien/state tax lien. Even though the land tax is also not Constitutional, it has been written into the State Codes in every State by statute, and is enforceable, unless you can prove your property has a "Land Patent". Whereas, the IRS liens, or State Tax Commission liens are not in the State Codes as statutes, and are not enforceable. The Counties and States try to say your land patent isn't in force because it was not issued by the original land owner, however this is not true, but turns out to be a wrestling match, proving it, however, the evidence is there.

The land tax follows the property, and the tax liens do not. A buyer of property at the closing must pay the prorated amount of property taxes, as also the seller must pay his share. Any lien from the IRS or state tax commission, are not mandatory, but they scare a lot of people into believing there are liens on the property. The liens from either of these two agencies, in due time will fall off.

You can come away from the IRS at any time, when you know the facts. No one needs to be afraid of these bullies. Don't give them jurisdiction and you have nothing to worry about, and you need not be afraid of them. There is a "Mistake" clause in the law, Federal Rules of Civil Procedure, Rule 60(b), if you do make mistakes. Everyone does. However, it does take a certain amount of courage, commitment, and faith in God to see you through. Many defenses to anything the IRS can accuse you for are mentioned in this book.

The questions you need to ask yourself when proceeding to resist the IRS are these: "How much do I believe in God, and His Son Jesus Christ?"; "Is what I know true or not?" and "How badly do I want to be free?" One of my favorite sayings I tell myself all of the time, when confronted with important personal decisions such as these are: "It is better to be dead right, than dead wrong".

*"7. Submit yourselves therefore to God. **Resist the devil**, and he will **flee** from you." "8. Draw nigh to God, and he will draw nigh to you. Cleanse your hands, ye sinners; and purify your hearts, ye double minded." "9. Be afflicted, and mourn, and weep: let your laughter be turned to mourning, and your joy to heaviness." "10. Humble yourselves in the sight of the Lord, **and he shall lift you up.**"* (James 4:7-10, KJV)

The biggest defense against the IRS is that it is a "rights issue", protected mainly by the Fifth Amendment. "It has long been established that a State may not impose a penalty upon those who exercise a **right guaranteed by the Constitution".** Frost & Frost Trucking Co. v. Railroad Comm'n of California, 271 U.S. 583. "Constitutional rights would be of little value if they could be indirectly denied, Smith v. Allwright, 321 U.S. 649, 644, or manipulated out of existence, Gomillion v. Lightfoot, 364 U.S. 339, 345,"

When you get a letter from the IRS, and with the knowledge you now have of who you are, you must respond, even if it is simply to write on the unopened letter, "REFUSED" "no such corporate person at this address, return to sender", then put it back in the mail box and send it back to them. This way they know your intent, that you understand, you are challenging the IRS's authority, and that the IRS authority does not apply to you. You must object to the IRS in a timely manner, because even in law, that which is not denied is the same as an admission. Keep copies of everything, even the fronts of the letters that you send back to them, that you have returned to sender.

Once again, this is a rights issue. Your defenses are: 1) You are not a corporate citizen, as you are a natural born, or naturalized citizen asserting your Common Law Rights, mainly the fifth Amendment, under the Constitution. 2) There is no law requiring you to file. 3) The 1040 form is a fraudulent form, and for you to file one, is to commit the felony of Mail-fraud, and the IRS cannot force you to commit a crime. 4) To file is a voluntary compliance system. 5) The remedy for opting out of the tax-payer status is at UCC 1-207/1-308 and UCC 1-103, and you are not liable for any unknown contracts/accounts, and you are not liable for the compelled benefit/fake money. 6) The IRS has no jurisdiction as you are under Common Law Jurisdiction, and the IRS is under Admiralty Jurisdiction. 7) The 16th Amendment does not apply to the natural born, or naturalized citizen, nor to businesses who are not incorporated.

Other than that, keep God in your heart, and your love for freedom, and treat the thieves like the criminals they are.

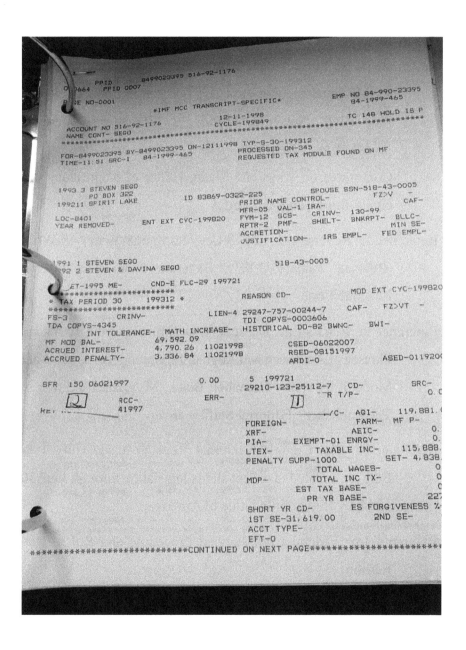

BIBLIOGRAPHY

Reference to: No Enforcement Statutes/IRS Regulations Applicable to Individual Income Tax! By: Eddie Kahn, 32504 Wekiva Pine Blvd., Sorrento, Florida, 32776 Internal Revenue Investigation, Hearings before a Subcommittee of the Committee on Ways and Mean, House of Representatives, eighty-third Congress. Part A.

Reference to: Reverse side of IRS Levy Form 668-W or 668-W(C), (Revised January 1983), Excerpts From The Internal Revenue Code.

Reference to: Black's Law Dictionary, Definitions of the Terms and Phrases of American and English Jurisprudence, Ancient and Modern, by Henry Campbell Black, M.A. Sixth Edition by The Publisher's Editorial Staff.

Reference to: The Complete Internal Revenue Code, July 1994 Edition, updated to reflect all tax legislation through June 30, 1994, by Research Institute of America.

Reference to: Federal Civil Judicial Procedure and Rules, 1997 Edition.

Reference to: Federal Rules of Criminal Procedure, Rule 54(5)(c).

Reference to: The Law That Never Was, by Bill Benson.

Reference to: The United States Constitution.

Reference to: Uniform Commercial Codes.

Reference to: Handbook For Special Agents, Criminal Investigation Intelligence Division, Internal Revenue Service, by Mortimer Caplin, Internal Revenue Service, Commissioner.

Reference to: 1040 Form of the Internal Revenue Service.

Reference to: 2555 Form, "foreign earned income"

Reference to: Chambers Encyclopedia, revised edition, volume III, New York, Collier Publisher, 1890, "D" volume.

Reference to: Standard Works of the Church of Jesus Christ of Latter-Day Saints, including the Bible, Book of Mormon, Doctrine and Covenants, and the Pearl of Great Price. Copyright 1979 by Corporation of the President of the Church of Jesus Christ of Latter-Day Saints, Salt Lake City, Utah, U.S.A., printed 1993.

Reference to: Whistle Blower, by Gene Corpening, by Alice Publishing, Granite Falls, NC. Published and copyright October 1998.

Reference to: The Ten Planks of the Communist Manifesto.

Reference to: Compendium of Studies of International Income and Taxes, 1979-1983, Statistics of Income, Internal Revenue Service.

Reference to: "International Income and Taxes", "Foreign Income and Taxes", Reported on "Individual Income Tax Returns" 1972-1978, Statistics of Income, Supplemental Report. By the Internal Revenue Service, publication 1108(4-81), "1975 Instructions for Form 1040 And for Schedules A, B, C, D, E, F, R, and SE"

Reference to: Titles of United States Codes, Office of the Law Revision Counsel, United States Codes, uscode.house.gov.

Reference to: The truth is in the Federal Register, letter to Richard Durjak, dated May 16, 1994.

Reference to: Letter from Pat Danner, Congress of the United States, dated September 12, 1996.

Reference to: Investigative Report, by William Cooper.

Reference to: Poem: I Am Just One Man, by Jay Merrell.

Reference to: Poem: The Bridge Builder, by Will Allen Dromgoole, from the Book: Best Loved Poems, Garden City publishing, Garden City, New York.

Reference to: The Declaration of Independence, July 4th, 1776

Reference to: Rendering Caesar His Due, by Sam Adams.

INDEX

Printed in the USA
CPSIA information can be obtained
at www.ICGtesting.com
CBHW050632061124
16957CB00007B/721